Coffee with God and Joy in the Winter Mornings

90 SIPS OF STRONG GRACE, BOLD FAITH, AND ENDLESS MERCY

DEBB JOY

DEEP
WATERS
BOOKS

Coffee with God and Joy in the Winter Mornings: 90 Sips of Strong Grace, Bold Faith, and Endless Mercy

Copyright © 2026 Debb Joy

Published by Deep Waters Books, P.O. Box 692301, Orlando, FL 32869

www.deepwatersbooks.com

Cover Design: June Hardee

Illustrations: Madolyn Phillips

First Printing 2025

Printed in the United States of America

Identifiers: 978-1-956520-17-0 (Hardcover) | 978-1-956520-18-7 (paperback) | LCCN 2025927515

Publisher's Cataloging-in-Publication data

Names: Joy, Debb, author.

Title: Coffee with God and joy in the winter mornings: 90 sips of strong grace, bold faith, and endless mercy / Debb Joy.

Description: Orlando, FL: Deep Waters Books, 2025.

Identifiers: ISBN: 978-1-956520-17-0 (hardcover) | 978-1-956520-18-7 (paperback) | LCCN 2025927515

Subjects: LCSH Christian women--Prayers and devotions. | Christian life. | Bible--Study and teaching. | Faith. | Suffering--Religious aspects--Christianity. | Bereavement--Religious aspects--Christianity. | Grief--Religious aspects-- Christianity. | Consolation. | Devotional calendars. | Meditations. | BISAC RELIGION / Devotional | RELIGION / Christian Life / Personal Growth | RELIGION / Christian Life / Death, Grief, Bereavement | RELIGION / Christian Life / Women's Issues

Classification: LCC BV4844 .C544 2019 | DDC 242/.643—dc23

Endorsements

Debb Joy is the real deal. I've seen her in the deepest of grief and the highest of joys, and she continues to be a faith-filled, encouraging disciple of Jesus. Once her pastor—I'm now her student. She draws me closer to the Savior with every devotional.

No fluff—straight to the heart. Get ready for God to work on you because the Spirit speaks through Debb Joy!

~ Reverend Leo Wideman, Kerrville, TX

A "happy-happy" faux-Christian—Debb Joy is NOT! Her faith is real, refined, and tempered in the crucible of a life filled with more than her share of loss, challenges, and reversals. Yet, there she remains—a light that brings us back from the abyss to God's unfathomable love and grace.

~ Harold Skaggs Jr., MD, Elder
Leader of Men in the Word Bible Study, Austin, TX

Coffee with God *starts daily by genuinely delighting in the Lord's presence. Debb Joy is a true servant who has faithfully used her gifts to bring him glory and further the kingdom.*

~ Savannah Chambers, Office Manager
First Baptist Church Sonora, Sonora, TX

Debb Joy is a force of nature. I have known her all of my life, and two of her traits have stood out consistently in all circumstances: her love for the Lord and her love of life and people. She stands with "one foot raised," ready to respond to the Lord's call with joy and passion wherever she is led. Debb is a treasure and a gift!

~ Jan Morrow Skaggs, Elder
Teacher of Lamplighters Bible Study, Austin, TX

To those who seek to love God big and run daily after our Lord, give them a copy of this devotional. Debb's devotion to Jesus, along with her personal life, struggles, and victories, gives her a unique, grace-filled perspective on faith, hope, and how to walk with Jesus.

Debb, my sister in Christ, mentor, and dear friend, is a great encourager in the faith. She has inspired me to grow spiritually, love others, and find joy in the Lord's presence. She walks through the wilderness with you and kneels fervently in daily prayer in her real prayer closet. Join her in the prayer closet and find peace, hope, and joy in Jesus.

~ Kristy D. Edwards, MD, CWS-P, FAAFP
Shannon Family Medicine Residency Program Director
Primary Care and Rural Medicine, School of Medicine
Texas A&M University

It would be hard to find a better person than Debb Joy to guide us into a deeper relationship with the Lord. Through her personal experiences, wisdom, and humor, we are drawn into the wisdom of her daily devotionals, creating a desire for more of the Lord's presence in our lives.

~ Carolyn Price, Director of Children's Choir
First Presbyterian Church, Midland, TX

I am blessed to know Debb as a fellow prayer warrior, Sunday school teacher, mentor to many, fireball of a friend, servant, and sister in Christ. I know firsthand that her heart is always seeking, listening, and obeying the Lord. Her last name, Joy, also perfectly describes her personality: sharing joy with others.

For the last several years, I have had the privilege of waking up each morning to a text message of Scripture and a devotional message from Debb. These started several years ago when she knew I needed them the most. I am one of many who have the privilege to receive these daily encouragements. She shares meaningful lessons that are sincere, Spirit-led, sometimes humorous and serious, but ALWAYS applicable.

Now, with this wonderful book, you can share in Debb's "Joy" with the most heartfelt of her daily devotions. Spend time with the Lord each day reading each message, and you, too, will learn more about God's Word, Debb's heart, and her mission to share his Word with others.

~ Shelly Shannon, Retired Public School Teacher
Sonora ISD, Sonora, TX

Debb is inarguably the most joyful person I have ever met. Her ability to encourage people by using the Word of God is unparalleled. I consider myself blessed to be her pastor and see her faith lived out daily.

~ Matt Killough, Senior Pastor
First Baptist Church, Sonora, TX

Contents

Dedication

I lovingly dedicate this book
to the love of my life,
my husband Kerry,
who makes my heart skip a beat
and leap for joy.

Thank you all for reminding me daily,
that having somewhere to go is home;
having someone to love is family;
and to have both is a blessing.

You are my blessing in this life.

In loving memory of my
Carmen Joy (1977–2011)

From the Heart

In February of 1977, I gave birth to our firstborn, a beautiful auburn-haired baby girl, Carmen Joy. Like any newlywed couple, my husband and I were ecstatic and envisioned the beginnings of our fairy tale—a happily married couple, the addition of more babies, a new puppy, and a small house that we called home.

Within eight months of our precious infant's birth, Carmen was diagnosed with cystic fibrosis. Devastation set in for both my husband and me. I drew from the same fount of strength I gulped from in my youth.

When I was a child, my mother had taught me the art of journaling. Throughout my high school years, I spent hours recording my most intimate thoughts concerning life's hard knocks, heartbreaks, cheerleader tryouts, boyfriends, jealousy, envious friends, and disappointments. Now, watching my young baby struggle, I turned my thoughts into written prayers. The years of practice spent recording the drama of high school now became my lifeline. Little did I know as I recorded my deepest pain, these words and times with my eternal Father would get me through the darkest days of my adult life. The joy of the Lord came every morning as I had my coffee with God.

Thirty-four years later, in 2011, our darling Carmen returned to our eternal Father. Years later, these four-seasonal devotionals, *Coffee with God and Joy in the Mornings: 90 Sips of Strong Grace, Bold Faith, and Endless Mercy*, are a reality.

I'm indebted to all those who contributed their experiences, joys, sorrows, moments of doubt, stories of unshakable faith, and testimonies. I pored over Sarah Young devotionals, books from the late Billy Graham and many others, including Max Lucado, and in them I found peace in God. I am so grateful for their obedience in writing down their faith-filled exhortations. I know I couldn't have gone through the fires of purification without their sweet words of encouragement.

To my amazing husband, my younger and extraordinary daughter, Madolyn Marie, and the many others who helped carry me through such sadness and darkness, I am so thankful for your love, support, and care. My amazing daughter, Madolyn, lovingly created each of these beautiful illustrations at the start of each month for all four 90-day devotionals.

I now believe more firmly than ever in the power of prayer. Most importantly, I am eternally grateful to God for the miraculous outpouring of grace, love, and faith he has lavished on our family and me.

From those whose paths we will probably never cross again, such as the doctors, nurses, and staff of Houston Methodist Hospital, to the people closest to me, please know that your unwavering faith and prayers have forged a deeper bond with my Savior that I never thought possible. My utmost appreciation to the special group that made this book come to fruition, especially Deep Waters Books, my publisher; my prayer warrior, and friend, Kim M. Clark; and Krista Murr, another devout prayer soldier and treasured friend, who, without her, these devotionals would have never made it into the right hands.

Of course, my most loving support team will forever be my family. My husband, Kerry, is my fiercest ally and has always allowed me to immerse myself in emotional experiences. My daughter, Madolyn, her husband, and my two handsome grandsons have been a constant and faithful source of strength in my daily life. I'm personally honored to have this book's illustrations brought to you, the reader, from my grandson and his gifted mother.

I pray Carmen's favorite verse comforts you and your family as it has us for so many years: "'For I know the plans I have for you,' declares the LORD, 'plans to prosper you and not to harm you, plans to give you hope and a future'" (Jeremiah 29:11 NIV).

Love, joy, and peace,

Debb Joy

Winter

Winter is one of my favorite seasons.
I love the smells of holidays, especially Christmas.

Even though Texas winters can be cold,
the warmth from my family melts
all disagreements and conflicts.

Grab your favorite hot drink and
curl up in a comfy chair
as we dive deep into
God's Word each day.

December

December 1

GRAB ON TO GOD'S LINE

The Lord isn't really being slow about his promise,
as some people think.
No, he is being patient for your sake.
He does not want anyone to be destroyed,
but wants everyone to repent.
~ 2 Peter 3:9

Patience isn't easy for most of us. If my plane is delayed a few minutes or something doesn't happen exactly when or how I expected it to, I can get impatient and frustrated.

Around us, I watch how the farmers wait for the land to yield its valuable crop and how patient they are for the autumn and spring rains. Their steadfastness and long-suffering convict me.

God knows the final product of what is happening to us, and despite what we prefer, he sears patience to our faith.

Like a lifeline, God offers his salvation to all who are in peril. Some reach out and grasp his line, freely receiving the gifts of Christ. Others, however, choose to ignore it, convinced they are safe without him. Tragically, they are lost for all eternity, having chosen the fleeting comforts of the world over the eternal promise of God.

Redeeming Lord, I lift up all those, especially my family
and loved ones, who have not yet made the life-changing
decision to follow you. Guide them toward your light
and help them to see the urgency of your call.
Time is short, and the stakes
are eternal.

December 2

IT COULD HAVE BEEN WORSE!

Let the peace of Christ rule in your hearts,
since as members of one body
you were called to peace.
And be thankful.
~ Colossians 3:15 NIV

As a junior in high school, I was a sprinter on the track team. Short-distance races were my forte. One afternoon, Coach Helmers approached me with a request: he needed a long-distance runner. Shocked that anyone could think that my 5'1" frame, with legs barely longer than a ruler, and plenty of extra weight on them, would be good for long-distance races, I respectfully told him, "I'm not your girl."

But I lost that battle. With some coaxing from my daddy, I decided to trust my coach and became the first leg of the mile relay. To my surprise, that junior year became a gift I never expected. Our team went on to win the state championship in several long-distance relays!

Our team of four runners and a determined coach resulted in achievements far beyond what I thought possible.

Looking back, I realize that if I had quit, I would have robbed myself of the blessing of thankfulness. Even when things seem wrong or beyond our ability, we can still trust God's guidance and thank him for the gifts he brings through unexpected challenges.

When Paul tells us to "let the peace of Christ *rule* in your hearts," this directive comes from the language of athletics. Our hearts are often the center of conflict, where feelings and desires clash—fear against hope, distrust against trust, jealousy against love. We are encouraged to let Christ's peace act as an umpire or referee in our hearts.

Lord, thank you for my unexpected challenges.
Teach me to trust your guidance
and to let your peace rule in my heart,
even when life feels overwhelming.
Help me to be thankful for
your work in every
situation.

December 3

I WON'T LET CIRCUMSTANCES TOUCH MY PEACE

I have told you these things,
so that in me you may have peace.
In this world you will have trouble.
But take heart!
I have overcome the world.
~ John 16:33 NIV

After walking with Christ for decades, I'm still amazed at how easily I rush into my busiest days without pausing to ask my heavenly Father to prepare me. Yet, my inner being doesn't need to be shaken by the demands before me or the messiness of the day. If only I would remember to root my spirit in Jesus each day, my day would go so much more smoothly, being grounded in eternity.

I'm starting to recognize that when anxiety begins to rise, I need to take a moment to detach myself from the noise and disturbances around me. Then to relax, breathe deeply, and remember: *no circumstance can disrupt God's peace.*

Jesus promises us, "My peace I leave with you; my peace I give to you. I do not give to you as the world gives" (John 14:27 NIV). Our Savior's peace is unshakable, untouched by the chaos of the world.

This promise of Christ's peace is for us today. We can trust in Jesus, for he has everything under control.

> *Lord, thank you for your perfect peace that surpasses all understanding.*
> *Help me to pause in the busyness of my day,*
> *surrender my worries to you,*
> *and trust in your unshakable control.*
> *May your peace fill my heart*
> *and mind as I walk through this*
> *and each day.*

December 4

WHO'S WRITTEN ON YOUR HEART?

"But this is the new covenant
I will make with the people of Israel after those days,"
says the LORD.
"I will put my instructions deep within them,
and I will write them on their hearts.
I will be their God,
and they will be my people."
~ Jeremiah 31:33

When our girls were toddlers, we would ask them, "Who's written on your heart?" They would always respond in glee, "Jesus!" Then, when they were preteens and teenagers, those declarations seemed so far away. Gratefully, that foundational truth returned to both of them as adults, and now with Madolyn as a parent.

The promise of a new covenant brought forth by the Son of God replaced the unattainable old one, which was broken by the people's disobedience. The foundation of this new covenant is Jesus Christ. Unlike the old covenant, which lacked the power to transform hearts or enable true obedience, the new covenant changes us from the inside out.

Until our hearts are renewed, we remain trapped in our same destructive acts, unable to break free. But Jesus, the Prince of Peace, shattered the prejudices of his day and continues to reach into our lives, transforming us by his love and grace. As long as sin exists, strife and contention will persist. Yet, when we surrender our lives to God, he writes his law on our hearts, giving us a deep, heartfelt desire to obey him.

Lord Jesus, I write you on my heart today.
Help me live for you, and deny sin and self-will.
Write and embed the Word of God
into my thoughts, being, and words.
Shape me to always reflect
your love and peace.

December 5

JESUS NEVER FORGETS

"Yes, I know," Boaz replied. "But I also know about everything you
have done for your mother-in-law since the death of your husband.
I have heard how you left your father and mother and
your own land to live here among complete strangers.
May the LORD, the God of Israel,
under whose wings you have come to take refuge,
reward you fully for what you have done."
~ Ruth 2:11–12

As a child, I always thought to be great, one must do
something of ultimate importance, like write the great
American novel, solve world hunger, or paint a masterpiece
—none of which, I must admit, I could ever do. At times, I can be
tempted by the lure of the world to think that public recognition
equals significance.

But the truth is, some of the most gratifying and meaningful deeds are
done quietly, with little or no recognition. On judgment day, Jesus will

reward those who scarcely remember the important acts they performed. Small gestures—sending a card to someone who needs encouragement, visiting a lonely shut-in, calling to show you care, or offering a glass of cool water in Christ's name—are the ones that matter most to our Lord and carry eternal significance.

These are the acts that Jesus honors, for they flow from hearts shaped by his love. As he said, "Blessed are the poor in spirit, for theirs is the kingdom of heaven" (Matthew 5:3 NIV).

God of Israel,
I pray that the blessings promised by you will
renew my strength this day.
Let me serve not for praise,
but with humble joy—
trusting that even the smallest acts
done in your name
hold eternal worth.

December 6

YOU'RE INVITED, COME ON IN!

Meanwhile, the disciples were in trouble far away from land,
for a strong wind had risen, and they were fighting heavy waves…
"Yes, come," Jesus said. So Peter went over the side of the boat and
walked on the water toward Jesus.
~ Matthew 14:24, 28–29

"Come!" Our Lord invites us.

Peter didn't need to be told twice. Not every day do you get the chance to walk on water through waves towering above your head to your Savior.

The first few steps went remarkably well. Then, a few strides in, Peter forgot to keep his eyes on the One who got him there in the first place. Suddenly, down he plunged into the deep, dark waves.

Peter knew better than to let arrogance keep him from screaming for help. His cry may have lacked finesse and wouldn't land him on the cover of *Sports Illustrated*, but he did what matters most: ask the only One who could help him.

Since Peter would rather swallow his pride than water, he shouted, "Save me, Lord!" (Matthew 14:30). Jesus reached out through the storm. A hand pierced the wind, rain, and waves, and the Son pulled up Peter, steadying the flaying disciple in his Master's embrace.

This message is unmistakable. If Jesus is just one of many options, then he is not the answer. If we think we can carry our burdens alone, we don't need a Burden-Bearer. And if we feel we can take him or leave him, we might as well leave him, because our Lord will not be taken half-heartedly.

> *Lord Jesus, just as you reached through the storm to rescue Peter,*
> *I pray you will demonstrate your power in my life.*
> *Help me trust you fully,*
> *knowing that with you,*
> *the laws of nature bend,*
> *burdens are lifted,*
> *and my faith is*
> *made strong.*

December 7

DO YOUR ACTIONS TELL A DIFFERENT STORY?

And so, dear brothers and sisters,
I plead with you to give your bodies to God
because of all he has done for you.
Let them be a living and holy sacrifice—
the kind he will find acceptable.
This is truly the way to worship him.
Don't copy the behavior and customs of this world,
but let God transform you into a new person
by changing the way you think.
Then you will learn to know God's will for you,
which is good and pleasing and perfect.
~ Romans 12:1–2

One of my favorite authors states, "We'll have three surprises in heaven: the people who we thought *would* be there *aren't there*, the people who we thought would *never* be there *are there*, and *we are there*."[1]

Only God can see our hearts. Others can't see what's happening inside of us. They don't know our thoughts, emotions, dreams, or motives. They can't see our inner commitment to Christ. All they can observe is our outward actions, and they often judge what's inside based on what's seen on the outside.

This is why Paul urges us to "present your bodies as a living sacrifice" (Romans 12:1 NKJV). The reason is simple: the way we use our bodies can cause others to stumble. How we dress, speak, and act signals to others what we truly are on the inside. Our outward behavior should consistently honor Christ and point others toward him.

Lord God, may my life—both inside and out—
be dedicated to your will.
Give me the courage and strength
to serve you in every thought, word, and action.
Help me to reflect your love
and grace to those
around me.

December 8

PRAYER IS NOT A ONE-AND-DONE ACTIVITY

Always be joyful.
Never stop praying.
Be thankful in all circumstances,
for this is God's will for you
who belong to Christ Jesus.
~ 1 Thessalonians 5:16–18

I must admit, I like getting things done. I think I get a dopamine rush each time I cross something off my to-do list—like I'm winning and not stuck in the same cycle.

Prayer is not a one-and-done activity. This discipline is an essential part of a healthy Christian life. Just like omitting a vital nutrient from our diet can make us physically weak, neglecting prayer leaves us spiritually anemic.

The command to "pray without ceasing" (v. 17) doesn't mean a quick, halfhearted prayer as we rush out the door each morning. Instead, we are called to dedicate intentional time to be alone with God—praying and listening as he speaks through his Word.

When we prioritize these moments of prayer, our minds and hearts become saturated with God's presence throughout the day. Even for the overworked mother, truck driver, construction foreman, or teacher, this practice is possible. A few quiet minutes with God—even in the cab of an eighteen-wheeler—can yield rich spiritual rewards. I've witnessed mighty-warrior truckers for the Lord who are making a profound difference, fueled by their dedication to prayer.

The beauty of prayer is that it's not confined to a single time or place. We can pray anywhere, anytime, and know that God hears us.

Patient and loving Father, may my life be saturated with
prayer today and always.
Help me to make time for you,
to listen to your Word,
and to trust that you
hear me wherever
I am.

December 9

JUDGED BY APPEARANCE OR BY THE HEART

But the LORD said to Samuel,
"Don't judge by his appearance or height,
for I have rejected him.
The LORD doesn't see things the way you see them.
People judge by outward appearance,
but the Lord looks at the heart."
~ 1 Samuel 16:7

Years ago, as a young mother, I had the joy of leading the singing for Vacation Bible School every summer. One of the children's favorite songs to act out was "There Once Was a Boy Named David"—the classic story of David and Goliath, brought to life with enthusiastic motions and joyful little voices.

As much as we love David's triumphant moment, the story leading up to it holds an important lesson. When Samuel went to anoint Israel's next king, their current King Saul—tall, handsome, and impressive—seemed to set the standard. Samuel might have looked for someone who fit the same mold, but God warned him not to judge by appearance.

God's standards aren't based on appearances. He sees our heart and judges by our faith and character. While everyone else sees your outward appearance, only you and God know what your heart looks like.

Lord, help me to focus less on what others see
and more on the state of my heart.
Teach me to grow in faith, love, and character,
that I might reflect your goodness
from the inside out.

December 10

THE PERPETUAL STOPWATCH

Understand this,
my dear brothers and sisters:
you must all be quick to listen,
slow to speak, and
slow to get angry.
~ James 1:19

I've noticed that as technology advances, my patience seems to decrease just as fast. Maybe it's just my hearing that's failing, as I find myself rudely interrupting my family members more frequently. We talk too much and listen too little, sending a subtle message: my ideas are more important than anyone else's.

For years, I loved James 1:19 (NIV): "Everyone should be quick to listen, slow to speak, and slow to become angry." Then one day, the Holy Spirit enlightened me on a deeper meaning of this passage and my enthusiasm took a nosedive. Suddenly, I felt faint, and honestly, I thought I might throw up.

Could it be that God is keeping a mental stopwatch on my conversations, tracking how much I talk versus how much I genuinely listen? James wisely challenges us to reverse the natural tendency to prioritize our own words.

Today, I find myself reflecting on this: When people talk with me, do they leave feeling like their viewpoints and ideas have value? Or do they walk away thinking I was more interested in my own thoughts?

> *Dear God, help me seek first to understand*
> *then to be understood, and most importantly,*
> *help me humbly listen to you first,*
> *then to those whom you put in my life.*
> *I pray this in Jesus's name.*

December 11

CAN YOU GRASP THE FULLNESS?

But he was pierced for our rebellion,
crushed for our sins.
He was beaten so we could be whole.
He was whipped so we could be healed.
~ Isaiah 53:5

I often wonder, would I give up *everything* in heaven to return to earth as an infant like Jesus did? Honestly, I'm glad God didn't ask me, because I would have said, "No!"

Jesus's earthly life began during persecution and peril. The Father sent him on a mission of love, mercy, and obedience. He even sent an angel to announce his conception and give him his name. After growing in the womb, like all other babies, the Son of the eternal Father, Jesus, became flesh in the likeness of man. The entire sky was filled with angelic beings proclaiming his birth. Magi traveled from kingdoms afar to bring him gifts fit for the most revered king on the planet.

Jesus was the most illustrious child ever born—the holy child of Mary, and the divine Son of God.

No sooner did he enter the world than Herod, being alerted of his birth, decreed Jesus's death. He murdered hundreds of infants and toddlers in an attempt to annihilate God's elected King. Jesus and his family escaped to Egypt until God called them back to Israel.

The Creator of the world grew up and experienced all the perils of humanity with all its infirmities, weaknesses, and capacity for suffering. His entire life paved the way to humiliation, torture, and the ultimate rejection by God, when he absorbed the entirety of God's wrath so we wouldn't have to.

Now Jesus is in heaven and is no longer limited by time and space. We won't fully grasp all that Christ gave up to come to earth until we see heaven for ourselves.

Lord, help me always remember
the fullness of the sacrifice
you made on the cross for us.
Thank you for coming down
from heaven for me.

December 12

SATAN'S FAVORITE WEAPONS

See, God has come to save me.
I will trust in him and not be afraid.
The LORD God is my strength and my song;
he has given me victory.
~ Isaiah 12:2

I can't tell you how many times I've seen, heard, and read in books and even the Bible, "Trust in God, and don't be afraid." For me, that command is easier said than done.

Many of us engage in some form of physical exercise to stay healthy. In the same way, God wants us to view trials as spiritual exercises designed to strengthen our trust muscles. These exercises prepare us for the fierce spiritual battles we face every day. One of Satan's favorite weapons in these battles is fear, aiming to paralyze us and keep us from living fully in faith.

But God has given us the tools to resist. His Word says, "Resist the devil, and he will flee from you" (James 4:7 NIV). How do we do that?

One way is to speak or sing praises to God. Worship is a powerful weapon that drives fear away and invites the presence of his peace. When you lift up praise, I promise you will feel our Father's warmth surrounding you.

And here's the greatest truth of all: the verdict is already in. You have been judged—*not guilty*—for all eternity because of Christ. We get to trust Jesus and not be afraid.

Lord, help me to trust you in every trial,
knowing that you are using these moments
to strengthen my faith.
Teach me to resist fear with praise
and to rest in the truth of my salvation
through Jesus Christ.

December 13

THERE IS NONE OTHER LIKE ME

There is no greater love than
to lay down one's life for one's friends.
You are my friends if you do what I command.
~ John 15:13–14

My husband and I have always taught our girls, and now our grandsons, to think of Jesus Christ as their "best friend"—or nowadays, their "bestie." We have explained that sometimes we are lucky enough to experience the love of a best friend in the flesh—someone who stands by us through life's ups and downs. But Jesus Christ is our most faithful companion. He will never leave us nor forsake us regardless of the cost. Our Savior walks hand in hand with us through every moment of our lives. And during the hard times, he even carries us.

Whatever today holds—pleasures, hardships, adventures, or disappointments—invite Jesus to share those moments with you. In this special friendship, you'll find that he offers practical and down-to-earth guidance for life's challenges.

Jesus has equipped each of us to remain conscious of his presence, even as we walk along the dusty paths of daily life. Nothing is ever wasted when shared with a best friend like him.

Lord Jesus, thank you for walking alongside me
as my constant companion and friend.
Help me to share every moment with you
and to trust your wisdom
and love in all things.

December 14

MAKE PRAYER A WAY OF LIFE

Pray in the Spirit at all times and
in every occasion.
Stay alert and be persistent in your prayers
for all believers everywhere.
~ Ephesians 6:18

A s a new believer, I didn't fully understand what it meant to "stay alert and be persistent in your prayers for all believers everywhere" (Ephesians 6:18). *How could anyone possibly be alert and pray persistently at all times? I wondered. When would we sleep?*

Now I get it. Years later, with a bit more spiritual maturity, I have made brief prayers throughout the day a cherished habit. It's amazing how God responds to every situation when I remember to invite him into my daily life. These simple moments of prayer might be asking for guidance in a challenge or spontaneously thanking him for last night's refreshing rainfall.

In today's world, where we face so many challenges and uncertainties, we need God's influence more than ever. We are called to pray—not just for ourselves, but for all believers in Christ and the church universal.

We must be alert and observant to the needs of others, and through prayer, we join God's work, trusting that he is ever-present and all-powerful.

Lord, teach me to turn to you throughout my day—
in moments of need, gratitude, and reflection.
Help me to lift up others in prayer,
trusting in your mighty power
to work in their lives and
in your church.

December 15

AVOID FOOLISH RISKS

Accept other believers
who are weak in faith,
and don't argue
with them about
what they think is right or wrong.
~ Romans 14:1

Wow. Don't argue with others about being right or wrong? Can I influence others for good instead of being influenced by them? I am sure I can't do any of those things. I can't do anything without my Savior. These are questions I've asked myself during different seasons of life.

The truth is, we all have areas where we are strong and others where we are weak. Our faith is strong in areas where we can engage with others—even those in sin—without falling into their patterns. But our faith may be weak in areas where we must avoid certain activities, people, or places to protect our spiritual lives.

I've found myself in both situations, and each has taught me the importance of self-awareness. Taking a spiritual inventory can help us recognize our strengths and guard against our weaknesses. It's not about perfection but about leaning on God for the wisdom and strength to navigate life with integrity.

Today, let's take time to ask God for his strength and to fill us with his Holy Spirit. Then for the strength to go forth, confident in his power, and be strong in the Lord.

Lord, help me to recognize both my strengths and weaknesses.
Fill me with your Holy Spirit so I can stand firm in faith,
resist temptation, and be a light to those around me.
May my life reflect your
strength and grace.

December 16

A MONSTROUS STEPCHILD

But when I am afraid,
I will put my trust in you.
~ Psalm 56:2

Have you ever hidden from fear or pretended you weren't anxious or afraid? Or even lied about it? I know I have.

They say "misery loves company," and fear is no exception. When we bury anxiety in the far recesses of our hearts, it often gives birth to fear—a monstrous stepchild we'd rather not claim!

But God, in his love and mercy, invites us to bring our anxieties into the light of his presence. There, with his help, we can confront and overcome fear. No longer do we have to dodge the enemy's fiery darts of fret and worry that plague us day and night.

Instead, we are called to trust in God, letting go of fearfulness one step at a time. As we focus on his goodness and faithfulness, the negativity that once gripped our hearts begins to loosen its hold. Gradually, peace replaces fear, and trust becomes our anchor.

Lord, I bring my fears and anxieties into your light today.
Help me to trust you fully, knowing that you are greater
than any worry that seeks to overwhelm me.
Replace my fear with peace, and
teach me to rest in
your presence.

December 17

CHRIST CHANGED ALL THAT

A servant of the Lord must
not quarrel but must be kind to everyone,
be able to teach,
and be patient with difficult people.
~ 2 Timothy 2:24

Over the years, I found that whether I'm teaching Sunday school, leading a Bible study, or sharing devotions with our family, it's more important to remember to listen carefully to others and their questions.

Servant leadership is patient and respectful and avoids getting tangled in unnecessary quarrels. True teaching and leading reflects Christ's love, as he commanded us with what we now refer to as the Golden Rule: "Love your neighbor as yourself" (Matthew 19:19 NIV).

Paul's advice to Timothy—and to all who teach God's truth—is simple yet profound: be kind and gentle. Good teaching does not promote squabbles or foolish arguments. Instead, it seeks to guide with patience, respect, and love.

This Golden Rule teaching implores us to treat others as we wish to be treated. Kindness isn't just for those who think like us or agree with us. It extends to the neighbor who doesn't maintain their yard the way you'd prefer or the coworker with a different perspective. Or the angry person driving on the road today.

Lord, teach me to reflect your kindness and love in all my interactions.
Help me to listen with patience, avoid unnecessary quarrels,
and extend grace to everyone I meet.
May others see your heart
in my actions today.

December 18

FOLLOW THE STAR

"We have never heard anyone speak like this!"
the guards responded.
~ John 7:46

Since so much of life is out of my control, one would think I would have mastered the art of trusting and obeying God. But no, I still struggle in this area. I can only imagine the immense amount of faith and trust both the shepherds and the wisemen needed to follow the star. I'm sure they, just like the temple guards, were in awe of God showing up through the natural.

From the moment of his birth, Jesus was recognized as the Messiah—and people wanted him dead. As an adult, he had his life repeatedly threatened by religious leaders. His words healed the blind, forgave sins, and raised the dead, yet his own family did not believe in him. He was betrayed by those closest to him.

Despite Jesus being God in the flesh, his life as God's Son was anything but easy. When we face difficult times, Jesus knows exactly how we feel. Will we always enjoy comfort as followers of Jesus? No. Even the most devoted saints face problems, temptations, and feelings of desolation. Many mature believers have left lucrative businesses, careers, and comforts behind to follow Christ in complete obedience.

All we need to do is follow the star. Just as it led the wise men to Christ, it leads us to the source of all comfort and eternal life today. As Queen Lucy in the *Narnia* series stated, "Once in our world, a stable had something in it that was bigger than our whole world."[1]

Lord, help me to wait patiently for you
and trust your plan, even when the path is difficult.
Strengthen me with courage and grace
to follow you each day.
During this season,
may I make time to celebrate your presence
in my life and share your love
with others.

December 19

IS THERE ROOM IN YOUR HEART?

She gave birth to her firstborn, a son.
She wrapped him in cloths and
placed him in a manger,
because there was no guest room
available for them.
~ Luke 2:7

I recall a Christmas years ago when I was so caught up in the hustle of shopping, decorating, and planning that I barely paused to reflect on the reason for the season. Late one evening, as I wrapped gifts in exhaustion, my youngest came over and asked, "What are we doing to celebrate Jesus's birthday?"

That simple question stopped me in my tracks. I realized how much room I had made for everything else, yet how little I had made for him. Convicted, my mind raced, *What? No room for Jesus? No room for the King of kings? No room for the Creator of the universe? But I have plenty of room for others.*

Sadly, I realized how little humanity has changed since that Bethlehem night over two thousand years ago. God is still on the fringes of most of our lives. We fit him in only when it is convenient for us, but we become irritated when he asks us to obey him or think he needs something. We might not say it, but our actions declare, "There's no room for you here, Lord."

God demands nothing from us. He just asks us to believe in his Son, Jesus, as our Lord and Savior. What seems so bizarre to me is that Jesus Christ, the Son of God, longs to share in and to be the source of the laughter and joy we all too rarely know. The most powerful being in the universe wants a personal relationship with each one of us.

Jesus Christ, as I am one of your children,
let my heart and actions
always declare there is room for you in my heart.
Help me remember
that you are the reason
for the season.

December 20

BUT IT CAME WITH A PINK BOW!

My soul thirsts for God,
for the living God.
~ Psalm 42:2 NASB

When I turned nine, the very thing I had been asking for stood outside our driveway with a beautiful pink bow draped over the handlebars.

My eyes almost bulged out of their sockets as I saw the prettiest pink bicycle with silver-sparkled spokes. I couldn't stop jumping up and down in delight. Gushing, I thanked my parents over and over again for the greatest gift *ever*!

Years later, my mother reminded me that the things of this world—the things we think we need—like my pink bicycle that I only rode a *total* of forty-eight hours in my life, pale in comparison to the greatest gift I had received: Jesus Christ!

These words of the psalmist might sound strange to most people today—"thirsts for the living God." We live in an age preoccupied with worldly possessions, and an eternal God seems almost irrelevant. Even if we refuse to admit it, the things of this world will never satisfy the longings of our souls.

Only God can meet our deepest yearnings. Pondering these truths, I become convicted especially during the Christmas season. What is crowding out my yearning for God in my life?

How about you?

> *God, reveal to my heart what crowds you out of my life.*
> *Help me repent and turn from all idols in my life.*
> *I pray that only you,*
> *the living God,*
> *will satisfy all my needs.*

December 21

YOU ARE ROYALTY

But you are not like that,
for you are a chosen people.
You are royal priests, a holy nation,
God's very own possession.
As a result, you can show others the goodness of God,
for he called you out of the darkness into his wonderful light.
~ 1 Peter 2:9

During the craziness of the holidays, the smell of pine reminds me of our family trip over the summer when we basked in the beauty of God's majestic creation—the Davis Mountains. I used to climb these same peaks as a child. Remembering the sweetness and purity of leaving the world and its problems at the foot of the mountain gave me a breath of fresh air and a calming sense of peace.

Now I want to bottle up that mountain, with all its grandeur, grace, and serenity, and carry it to my backyard and drink its beauty in each day. And in a way, I can. As I walk through my days, I can continually look to my Creator and communicate with him. His presence, like those mountains, offers peace, strength, and a reminder of his power and love. Through prayer and his Word, I get to quiet my mind, as the Holy Spirit prepares me for each day ahead.

When things get hectic, we need to remind ourselves who we belong to. We are sons and daughters of the King of kings—royalty in his kingdom, his beloved children.

Lord, please forgive me when I focus more on the chaos of life
and forget to come to you, my King,
for my daily in-filling of fresh wind and
strength to face my day.
Help me remember to seek you,
your strength, and your
face always.

December 22

UNDERSTANDING JOY THROUGH GRIEF

Be thankful
in all circumstances,
for this is God's will
for you who belong to Christ Jesus.
~1 Thessalonians 5:18

"To survive grief is to understand joy. Joy comes from understanding that God keeps his promises no matter the circumstances." Those words pierced my heart, spoken by a grieving mother who recently lost her college-age son to a heinous act of violence.

Paul reminds us in Scripture that we are not called to thank God *for* everything that happens to us but rather to thank him *in* everything. Evil does not come from God, and we should not attribute it to him. But even in the midst of evil and tragedy, we can be thankful for his unshakable presence and for the good he can bring out of the pain.

The same mother shared with me another truth from her heart: "I know that I have a battle in front of me. I hurt. I grieve. This makes me love harder."

As a mother who also buried one of her children, I understood her pain, even though her words challenged me. To show respect for such great loss, may we also learn to love harder—to cherish those around us and to let our love shine brightly in a world often overshadowed by darkness.

Lord, amid grief and pain,
teach me to find joy in your promises.
Help me to trust in your presence and
the good you can bring from even
the darkest situations.
May I give thanks in all circumstances
and honor those who suffer loss
by loving harder,
just as you
love us.

December 23

CALMLY, TRUST ME!

Crop failure and the death of animals
would devastate Judah.
But Habakkuk affirmed
that even in times of starvation and loss,
he would still rejoice in the LORD.
When nothing makes sense and
when your troubles seem to be more than you can bear,
remember that God gives strength.
~ Habakkuk 3:17–19

Being I was raised in a small West Texas town, everyone I grew up with knows all too well the devastation of prolonged drought on a farmer's crop or the ravages of anthrax on a rancher's cattle. These struggles can make us wonder why hardships come, especially to those striving to live righteously.

In today's Scripture, the prophet Habakkuk asks God why evil people prosper while the righteous suffer. God's answer? They don't, at least not in the long run. God sees every detail, and the world remains firmly under his authority. While we cannot always see what God is doing—or what he will do—our role is simpler than we make it.

We are called to do the next best thing, stay in tune with God, remain thankful, and rest in his sovereign control. I find that the older I get, the more I tend to make things far too complicated. I watch myself and others try to fix the problem ourselves, instead of trusting God, shouldering burdens we were never meant to carry.

Let's choose to trust God today, no matter the droughts or hardships we face, knowing that his plan is perfect and his authority is absolute.

Dear God, keep my gaze fixed on you
in seasons of drought or plenty and sickness or health.
Help me remember you are sovereign and in control.
Give us your strength.
Remind me that you see
and know all things and that your justice
will prevail in your time.

December 24

IN THE TRENCHES, WHAT DO YOU HEAR?

Jesus said to the woman,
"Because you believed,
you are saved from your sins.
Go in peace."
~ Luke 7:50

During the First World War, on Christmas Eve, an extraordinary stillness fell over the battlefield. As soft snow blanketed the ground, the thoughts of young soldiers turned toward home and their loved ones.

In the quiet, one soldier began to hum "Silent Night." Slowly, others joined in until the trenches were filled with the familiar carol. When they finished, they were astonished to hear the song echoing from the enemy trenches across no-man's-land, sung in their native tongue. That night, amid the darkness of war, the world experienced a moment of peace. Hearts turned toward the Prince of Peace, the Christ of Christmas.

How different our world could be if, this very morning, we united our hearts in one accord. When Christ is near, discord turns to harmony, and chaos gives way to calm. Earth can begin to reflect heaven when we welcome the peace of Christ into our lives and share it with others.

As we celebrate Christmas, let us be reminded that full peace will come only when Christ returns. Until that glorious day, may we strive to be messengers of his peace in our homes, communities, and world.

May the Prince of Peace reign in my heart,
and in my family's, this season.
Help me always go in peace
and bring your light to a world in need.
I praise you, Jesus Christ, my Savior,
as I celebrate the eve
of your birth.

December 25

FIRST CHRISTMAS

The thief's purpose is to steal and kill and destroy.
My purpose is
to give them a rich and satisfying life.
~ John 10:10

Merry Christmas! This day is not just a date on the calendar. This birthday is far more than an annual holiday or a day to glorify selfishness and materialism.

Christmas is a celebration of the event that caused heaven to sing with joy. It is the story of a specific time, in a specific place, when a specific person was born. This infant was and *still is* "God of God, Light of Light, very God of very God,"[1] our Lord, Jesus Christ. Our King left the comforts of eternity and sweet communion with the Father to be born an infant in a sinful world, live a perfect life, and then die in our place for our sins.

This sacrifice by our Savior is reflected in a horrific, well-organized killing machine. By July 1941, the Nazis congratulated themselves on their efficiency at Auschwitz. Yet, prisoners from the work side of the camp occasionally found ways to escape. One night, after such an event, the guards sought vengeance by condemning several prisoners to death.

A frail priest stepped forward and said softly, "I would like to die in place of the one you have condemned to death, for I am old and good for nothing. My life will serve no purpose."

That man, Father Kolbe, gave his life so another might live. His sacrifice became a symbol of hope to the broken hearts in Auschwitz. Father Kolbe's love reflects the greater sacrifice of Jesus Christ, who gave his life to bring hope to a world lost in sin. This is the true meaning of Christmas—not gifts or decorations, but the birth of the Savior of the world.

Prince of Peace, you are our faithful shepherd.
This Christmas,
I put my trust in you,
the hope of the world.
Let me remember and worship you,
the true meaning
of Christmas.

December 26

WAIT QUIETLY FOR OUR LORD

So, it is good to wait quietly for salvation from the LORD.
And it is good for people to submit at an early age
to the yoke of his discipline.
~ Lamentations 3:26–27

The day after Christmas can be filled with returning materialistic gifts that don't fit, don't work, or we don't need. Instead of running out to spend that gift card, I wonder what today would be like if we, just like Mary, sat by the manger and stared at our King. As a mother inhales the "neck sugar" of her newborn, may we just sit, basking in the presence of our Emmanuel.

That quiet submission, trusting in the yoke of our Father's discipline, is true worship and produces a bountiful harvest of eternal fruit in our lives. The familiar and beloved declaration, often echoed in worship, would be our mantra: "Great is his faithfulness; his mercies begin afresh every morning" (Lamentations 3:23).

As we "submit to the yoke of his discipline" (Lamentations 3:27), we willingly yield to God's teaching through the trials we face. That involves silently reflecting on God's character and works, repenting with humility, and practicing confident patience as we trust his timing.

Christ alone remains the answer in a world that feels increasingly disorderly, dangerous, and ungovernable. He carries the burdens of our hearts and offers hope to a seemingly hopeless world. Even in the midst of turmoil, we can rest in this truth: there is bright hope for tomorrow.

Lord, thank you for your faithfulness and
mercies that are new every morning.
Teach me to yield to your discipline,
grow in humility, and
trust you through every challenge.
Help me to find hope in you alone,
even when the world
feels overwhelming.

December 27

IT'S WORTH IT, EVERY DAY

So Jesus explained,
"I tell you the truth,
the Son can do nothing by himself.
He does only what he sees the Father doing.
Whatever the Father does,
the Son also does.
~ John 5:19

By now, many of you (like me) have thought, pondered, and deliberated over your New Year's resolutions. I usually start my own list in the week leading up to New Year's Eve, but all too often, I fail to follow through, leaving me frustrated and kicking myself year after year.

In the past several days, however, my thoughts have been far from resolutions. My heart has been heavy as I've prayed for and mourned for a couple I've never met—parents preparing to bury their beautiful daughter, killed in a tragic head-on collision shortly after celebrating

Christmas with her family. Christmas Day will never be the same for them. Whether five years or twenty-five years pass, they will forever carry the memory of *that* Christmas Day.

This has made me pause and ask myself, "Do I truly spend enough time among the suffering people of this world? How can I possibly meet the needs of those I don't even know?"

As my thoughts turn to Christ, I picture him walking among the suffering. Reflecting on his life, and all his miracles, I am in awe of him. Jesus didn't have to come down from his heavenly throne. Yet, he chose to walk this rugged landscape of pain, to be our Savior.

This Christmas season, let's focus on that precious baby born for us. Let's follow his example of how he walked among and offered deep compassion for the hurting.

Lord, help me see the needs of those who are suffering
and give me the courage to act.
With your help, use me to bring comfort
and hope to others,
as you have done
for me.

December 28

WE'VE BEEN GIVEN THE GREATEST GIFT

We have different gifts,
according to the grace given us.
~ Romans 12:6 NIV

Christmas is over. Some have already begun dismantling their decorations, and perhaps it hasn't even been seventy-two hours and you've had the experience of having young children complain about not receiving the gift they wanted or that they're bored with the ones they opened. Maybe you have already fought the day-after-Christmas retail return lines or bought all the 70 percent off Christmas sale items.

God our Father has given gifts to each of us, and I pray we may never become discontent or bored with them. The greatest gift of all time is that of his beloved Son. The Bible also teaches that God has given other gifts, ones that come from the Holy Spirit's ministry in our lives. We don't need to worry about those gifts we don't have. Instead, we should be grateful for those God has given us. We will never be more satisfied than when we are using our God-given gifts to fulfill his will in our lives.

Thank you, Lord, for giving each and every one of us
spiritual gifts. Provide hope to the hopeless,
healing to the sick, provision for those in want,
and comfort to the grieving.
Help me use my gifts for your glory
and to advance your kingdom,
not my earthly treasures.
Keep my focus on you and eternity,
not the flesh.

December 29

WHEN GOD SAYS NO

Then the Lord said, "Learn a lesson from this unjust judge.
Even he rendered a just decision in the end.
So don't you think God will surely give justice to his chosen
people who cry out to him day and night?
Will he keep putting them off?
I tell you, he will grant justice to them quickly!
But when the Son of Man returns, how many will he find
on the earth who have faith?"
~ Luke 18:6–8

There have been times in my life when I struggled to accept God's answer of "no." I sometimes even refused to take no for an answer, believing that if I prayed long and hard enough, God would eventually grant my request.

Growing up, I often heard my earthly daddy say, "Once and for all, the answer is no." And he meant it. Looking back, I can see the wisdom in those moments. My dad's nos weren't meant to hurt me but to guide me in the right direction.

In the same way, God's "no" is always given in love and wisdom, even when it's hard to understand. The purpose of prayer is not to conform God to our will but to align our will with His. True prayer changes us, teaching us to trust him, even when the outcome isn't what we hoped for.

Let's commit to developing a deeper reliance on God to guide us through our troubles and to trust his decisions completely—yes, even when his answer is "no" to our prayers.

Lord, teach me to trust you fully,
even when your answer is not what I want.
Help my will to align with yours and to grow in faith,
knowing that your plans are always for my good.
Give me peace and strength to accept your guidance,
even when it's hard
to understand.

December 30

MAY I RECOGNIZE THE WARNING SIGNS

Oh, how great are God's riches and
wisdom and knowledge!
How impossible it is for us
to understand his decisions and his ways!
~ Romans 11:33

As the end of another year approaches, people are already speculating about what the new year will bring. Yet, a year from now, most of those predictions will likely have completely missed the mark! I like to write them down and then review them a year later. My husband and I usually laugh over the disparity.

The truth is, no one knows the future—except God. As the world continues to uncover astonishing facts about politics, social media trends, health crises, and the universe itself, our knowledge remains minuscule compared to that of our heavenly Father.

God is infinite. He knows all because he created it all. While we grapple with confusion and uncertainty about the unknown, he stands sovereign and sure. As James reminds us, "How do you know what your life will be like tomorrow? Your life is like the morning fog—it's here a little while, then it's gone" (James 4:14).

This year, let our resolutions be different. Let's resolve to trust in the one and only God who knows your future and works all things for his glory. Trust him for all your tomorrows.

Dear Creator of the universe, keep my focus on you.
You are all-knowing, all-powerful, and all-present.
Help me trust in you and your plans,
even though I don't understand your ways.
I lay this next year on your altar.
Direct my paths.
My times are in
your hands.

December 31

PERFECT TUNING

For you are my hiding place;
you protect me from trouble.
You surround me with songs of victory.
~ Psalm 32:7 NASB

Are you desperate for something to change in your life next year? Since Christmas, have you been feeling weary and worn? Would I disappoint you I answered "yes" to both? Then perhaps I should have lied!

I read the other morning about an elderly man with a badly out of tune violin. Out of desperation, he called a local radio station to strike the musical tone "A" at precisely high noon. The station decided to accommodate the old fellow, and he tuned his fiddle perfectly.

Very much like the fiddle, when we live apart from God, our lives get out of tune and out of harmony with others. I have enjoyed spending time each day with you, my coffee, and God. As we begin the next year, may we ask God to help tune our lives every day to his Word. He has promised to be faithful. And for that, you can be certain of fine-tuning—God's perfect tuning.

As we cross the threshold into another year, I pray you will forever seek God's face through his Word and he will bless you with his peace that surpasses all understanding.

Dear God, keep me in tune with you.
Draw close to me and my loved ones
each and every day of the next year.
Keep me in your hiding place
and protect me from trouble.
Surround me with your songs of victory.
In Jesus's precious name
I pray.

January

January 1

REVELATION . . . OUR HOMECOMING

He who is the faithful witness to all these things says, "Yes, I am coming soon!" Amen! Come, Lord Jesus! May the grace of the Lord Jesus be with God's holy people.

~ Revelation 22:20–21

Years ago, a senator asked the Reverend Billy Graham, "Are you a pessimist or an optimist?" He smiled and replied, "I'm an optimist." The senator continued, "Why?" Mr. Graham responded, "I've read the last page of the Bible."[1]

The Bible speaks of a heavenly city set upon a hill, whose builder and maker is God, where those redeemed will be superior to angels. It speaks of "a pure river of life, clear as crystal, and proceeding from the throne of God and of the Lamb" (Revelation 22:1).

As we step into another year, reflecting on the joys and disappointments of the past can be bittersweet. But instead of lingering in what has been, let us look forward with hope and resolve. We are encouraged to "be patient and stand firm, because the Lord's coming is near" (James 5:8 NIV).

The beginning of the year is an opportune time to follow in Billy Graham's footsteps and turn to the end of the Bible—Revelation. This book is not just a conclusion; it is the assurance of victory and the promise of the new life to come.

The comfort of knowing "the LORD shall reign forever and ever" (Exodus 15:8 NASB) gives us hope as we face the unknown of the coming year.

Mighty Counselor, thank you for the gift of worship and
the chance to begin a new year with hope rooted in your promise.
Guide me as I look forward to your return,
and help me live each day
with patient expectation
and unwavering faith.

January 2
WHAT IS YOUR HIGHEST JOY?

Acknowledge that the LORD is God! He made us, and we are his.
We are his people, the sheep of his pasture.
~ Psalm 100:3

Years ago, having others accept me was the pinnacle of true happiness. I wanted their approval so badly that it didn't matter whether I agreed with them or not; I found myself working overtime and unsuccessfully trying to please people.

At some point in our lives, we must decide what is our highest joy. Jesus tells us to "love the Lord your God with all your heart, and with all your soul, and with all your mind and with all your strength" (Mark 12:30 NIV).

As we grow up, we find delight in what we have, then as adolescents in what we do, and finally as adults in what we are. The child lives for possessions, the youth for experiences, and the adult for character. Every person has a perspective on life (depending on their stage) to seek their utmost happiness.

Abraham wanted, first and foremost, to please God. When he lifted his eyes, he saw the stars and all that God had made, and through his faith, he became a friend of God. He inherited the Promised Land, a family, and a nation, all prepared for him by his Creator.

Our joy must also be found only in God. We praise and trust God because he is holy, good, and perfect. What if our entire focus in life was to love the Lord with all our hearts, minds, souls, and strength? The world would be a very different place.

Dear God, give me a heart to love you with everything I have.
Let me receive the highest joy
knowing I am one of your sheep
and precious children.

January 3

DO YOU HAVE A PROBLEM?

Nothing in all creation is hidden from God.
Everything is naked and exposed before his eyes, and
he is the one to whom we are accountable.
~ Hebrews 4:13

L aughing and reveling, we recently celebrated my grandson's birthday. After returning home to continue the festivities, I realized I had left my wallet at the restaurant.

At first, a wave of calmness overtook me as I informed everyone of my missing wallet. And then anxiety sent me into a frantic tailspin. A friend called me, as if God had a direct line to my heart. She instinctively knew I was having a spiritual meltdown. Over the phone, she started praying for me and stopped my emotional tirade in midstream.

Life is difficult, and sometimes it can seem like we are in a cycle of endless problems. Do we moan and groan or face them? We're all given choices. It's our job to teach the next generation the discipline to accept and solve our problems, instead of encouraging them to run and hide from their troubles.

If we listen to the world, we will be enticed to run to a substitute, dismissing the fact that for each problem we encounter, there is a God-appointed instructor and solution ready for us. Remember that each trial is made to stretch and challenge us in our walk with our Creator.

Lord, thank you for being the one who sees every part of my life.
Help me to turn to you when problems arise,
trusting in your wisdom and provision.
Teach me to face my challenges with faith and courage,
knowing that you are always present
and in control.

January 4
THE GOD OF SECOND CHANCES

Now go and tell his disciples, including Peter,
that Jesus is going ahead of you to Galilee.
You will see him there, just as he told you before he died.
~ Mark 16:7

Does God give second chances to those who have failed him? Absolutely. We see this clearly in Peter's story. The very disciple Jesus called "the rock" on which he would build his church proudly proclaimed himself Jesus's most faithful follower. Yet, when Jesus faced his darkest hour, Peter denied knowing him—not once but three times. Peter's failure was so profound that he wept bitterly into the night.

There have been times when I've felt like Peter. Moments when I leaned on my pride instead of seeking guidance from my Counselor. Times when I faltered and sinned, disappointing not only myself but those around me, and, most of all, my God. And just like Peter, I cried over my mistakes and regrets.

God is our God of restoration. He desires to meet us where we are and guide us to where he wants us to be. Just as Jesus's first words to his disciples after the resurrection were words of peace, he offers the same to us after we stumble.

If you feel like you've failed your Lord, don't give up. Just as he did with Peter, Jesus stands ready to restore and develop you further. He is merciful and forgiving, always waiting with open arms for you to return and repent.

> *Lord, thank you for being the God of second chances.*
> *Help me come to you with a repentant heart,*
> *knowing you are ready to forgive and restore.*
> *Wipe away my guilt and fill me*
> *with your peace.*

January 5

A SURE THING

And this same God who takes care of me
will supply all your needs from his glorious riches,
which have been given to us in Christ Jesus.
~ Philippians 4:19

A s a toddler, when my daughter started to understand her cystic fibrosis diagnosis, she hated doing her daily physical therapy even though she desperately needed the specific movements to keep her healthy. She loathed the activity and the hard work. Had we listened to her and not the pulmonologists, she wouldn't have lived past the age of seven.

God longs to bless his children and bestow on them every good and perfect gift (see James 1:17). One lesson Jesus taught his beloved followers is to have confidence that God answers every petition.

Does that mean God gives us a blank check when we pray? Will our every wish be granted? No. Our Creator's love is far greater than that. God loves us enough to say, "Not yet, my beloved." Or "No, you can't have that, my child. Trust me." Sometimes the response is not what we seek.

Thankfully, our heavenly Father knows what is best for us and only provides what will make us stronger warriors for Christ. The closer we get to our eternal King in our walk of faith, the more our prayers will reflect his will.

To receive and enjoy God's abundant gifts, we must draw near to him, spend time in his Word, and obey his statutes—every day.

Father, give me the grace to walk in holy obedience
to your living Word, the Bible.
In Jesus's name, I pray.

January 6

HELP MY UNBELIEF

The father instantly cried out,
"I do believe, but help me overcome my unbelief!"
~ Mark 9:24

The account of the deaf and mute boy possessed by an evil spirit since early childhood (Mark 9:14–29) gives me pause. The desperate father brings his seizing son, who a demon had tried to destroy by throwing him into the fire and water, to the Savior of the world. The dad begged Jesus, "If you can do anything, have compassion on us and help us" (Mark 9:22 NKJV). The father believed that if there was any hope for his son, it lay with Jesus. And the Lord told him, "If you can believe, all things *are* possible to him who believes" (v. 23 NKJV).

Jesus then mercifully cast out the demon and healed the man's son.

I have often asked our great Healer to grant wellness to an individual. Sometimes God has answered my prayers, but countless times the healing occurred on the other side of eternity.

Faith does not come from ignorance. Instead, it is based on what we know. Before we believe in others with something precious to us, we first try to find out if they are trustworthy.

When you are struggling to believe, do not avoid your Savior. Jesus desires us to believe and trust in him despite the outcome. When we question our faith, perhaps we need to become more acquainted with him, his Word, and his promises.

Almighty God, strengthen my faith when I am weak.
Help me receive comfort from the truth
found in your Word.
In Jesus's name,
I pray.

January 7

RECEIVE IT SO YOU CAN SHARE IT

Now may our Lord Jesus Christ himself and God our Father,
who loved us and by his grace gave us eternal comfort
and a wonderful hope.
~ 2 Thessalonians 2:16

In reading this passage, I couldn't help but think of Noah. One can only imagine what must have gone through his mind when God gave him the plans for constructing an ark.

Once completed, God gathered a pair of every living animal and their significant other, as well as six-hundred-year-old Noah, his wife, his three grown sons, and their wives, and placed them in the ark. I can only imagine that parade of animals followed by the eight obedient humans that entered the ark on that day.

Our Father then closed the doors. With everyone safely inside, for the *first time* in all creation, the floodgates of heaven opened up and it rained—really hard. And if that wasn't enough, the springs of the great deep burst forth (Genesis 7:11), drowning the earth and all its mountains (Genesis 7:12–19) for forty days. Historians believe this group was on the ark for 371 days.[1] Then, after the second trip of a dove that returned with an olive branch—they finally had proof the waters were subsiding.

What an adventure! To all the "Noahs" of the world, to all who search the horizon for that fleck of hope, remember God came as a dove bearing a leaf—an encouragement to keep trusting in him. When given a sprig of hope from God, treasure it. Then as you're prompted, give it away in love to encourage someone else.

Dear loving Creator, thank you for loving me and
giving me the leaf of hope. Give me the wisdom and
discernment to pass on my branch of hope.
Allow me to be an instrument
of new beginnings.

January 8

A PROMISE TO CLING TO IN A HOSTILE WORLD

During my time here,
I protected them by the power of the name you gave me.
I guarded them so that not one was lost,
except the one headed for destruction,
as the Scriptures foretold.
~ John 17:12

The other morning, awakened by my trusty alarm, I felt a rush of excitement. What would my heavenly Father have in store for me today? By noon, clad in my armor of God, I was rebuking the darkness in the mighty name of Jesus and dodging flaming spiritual arrows from all directions. Unfortunately, not every day goes as victoriously!

The world is a battleground, a constant spiritual and physical war between good and evil. Jesus prayed that God would keep his people pure and give them abundant joy, peace, and protection from Satan's power.

Before we enter into battle, we need to pray. Jesus frequently prayed alone with his Father, separating himself from every distraction.

Trying to find that haven without interruption can be challenging at times. Maybe you can designate your favorite chair, a closet, the cab of a truck, or a walking path around your neighborhood (with or without your favorite four-legged friend) to spend time with the Lord.

Talk to God as you would a friend. Confess your fears and needs, and then worship your King in his creation. That may be all that is required to find your special time with your Maker.

Dear God, despite my busy schedule,
help me make room for our special time and place.
Pour out the comfort and peace from the Holy Spirit
as I cling to you, my Maker,
in the middle of my
spiritual war.

January 9
WHO'S THAT KNOCKING?

Surely righteous people are praising your name;
the godly will live in your presence.
~ Psalm 140:13

I 've often imagined what I would do if the Lord appeared at my door. I picture Christ standing there, clothed in a long white robe with a thick leather belt around his slim waist. His feet would be adorned with sturdy, worn sandals bearing the marks of countless miles traveled. His face would be smooth and unlined, framed by long, dark, wavy hair, and his eyes—a deep, loving, golden brown—would shine with kindness. I envision his smile peeking through a thick, flowing beard as he waits patiently for an invitation to enter my home and heart.

In that moment, I hope I would be at a loss for words—a rarity for someone like me who is known to be quite talkative. But I believe my only response would be an outpouring of worship: "You are worthy, my Lord, to receive glory, honor, and power."

Are you ready to invite Jesus into your home and heart? The time to prepare is now; don't put it off.

The day will come when the knock arrives, and I pray you will be able to respond with joy, "I've been expecting you, my Lord! Please, come into my home and heart."

Lord Jesus, prepare my heart
so that I am ready to receive you at any moment.
Let my life reflect the love and anticipation
I hold for you. May I always be willing
to open my door and
invite you in.

January 10

DO YOU BELONG TO A MODEL CHURCH?

We proudly tell God's other churches about your endurance
and faithfulness in all the persecutions
and hardships you are suffering.
~ 2 Thessalonians 1:4

When planning a big event, I experience all these emotions: excitement, insane busyness, and then exhaustion. Just recently, as I prepared for friends visiting for the weekend, I vacillated between being overwhelmed by everything I needed to accomplish and not getting anything done because I ran from one job to another.

Human nature tends to be one way or the other. We tend to either be so overly patient that we aren't aware, or so hyper-attentive that nothing gets done. Today's church has become a hybrid of the restless and the resting, resulting in a cluster of adults resembling squabbling preschoolers.

The Bible tells us the church in Thessalonica was a model. Somehow they got the message to be prepared for Jesus's second coming and they immediately started preparing. Some sold their homes. Others quit their jobs, and a few merely sat, twiddling their fingers while waiting for our Savior's return. Despite the persecution and severe suffering (see Thessalonians 1:6), these church members embraced the message of redemption by Jesus Christ. Their faith did not waver. This church exemplifies the kind of trust we as a church need today— a kind that perseveres no matter what is swirling around us.[1] Like Thessalonica, we all need an outpouring of encouragement, leadership, and eternally focused preaching.

Lord Jesus Christ, while I wait for your return,
help me to practice inspiring others
with renewed courage, spirit, and hope.
Place me in the church you want me in.
Give me the gift of perseverance
as I await your return
for everything.

January 11
THE FAITHFULNESS OF CHRIST

The Lord hears his people when they call to him for help.
He rescues them from all their troubles.
The Lord is close to the brokenhearted;
he rescues those whose spirits are crushed.
~ Psalm 34:17–18

In my walk with God, I have found that if I had never faced adversity for my faith, I would remain stagnant. Many times, through the sickness and death of our daughter, acts of betrayal, and the loss of close relationships, I have had to call out to God for help not to remain bitter.

As a believer, I have had to decide to trust Christ in every area of my life, despite the difficulties. If I had never gone through turmoil or sorrow, my interactions with God could be compared with that of a great-great-grandfather whom I'd heard stories about but never met. There would always be a sense of distance and some familiarity, but not an intimate connection.

This is not the kind of relationship God wants with his children. Our eternal Father went to great lengths to clear the way so that nothing stands between him and his beloved children, which is you and me.

The Creator of the universe longs for you to call out to your Father God, your Abba. Won't you ask God to reveal himself to you today?

Oh sovereign Lord, strengthen me.
Lift me up when I am faint-hearted.
Show yourself to me, one of your children,
as I call out to you, my Abba Father and God.
You are our great Shepherd.

January 12
HAVE YOU LOST YOUR SALTINESS?

You are the salt of the earth.
But what good is salt if it has lost its flavor?
Can you make it salty again?
It will be thrown out and trampled underfoot as worthless.
~ Matthew 5:13

"Yuck! So this is what food tastes like without salt," my friend's husband exclaimed during dinner. When his wife explained that she didn't salt his meal due to his high blood pressure, he shook his head and said, "I'd rather go on medication than eat like this the rest of my life!"

Salt is a powerful preservative. Spiritually, it makes us more like Christ. If we are not in the right relationship with our Lord, Jesus said we are like salt that has lost its saltiness and is therefore good for nothing.

How do we test our "saltiness"? We need to examine all aspects of our life. Are we protecting it from the destructive influences that surround it? Do sinful influences in our work environment halt because we are there? If people around us are deteriorating, we need to go to our Lord and ask him to adjust our lives so that we can be used to preserve others.

The presence of Christ activates his Spirit in you, making you like him. His power through your salvation can do amazing things—cure the addict, mend a broken home, heal the pain of the past, restore a wayward child, and comfort a grieving heart. All this is available to you and those around you as Christ lives in and works through you.

Forgiving and loving God,
may I never lose my saltiness.
Use me as a tool in your hands!
You have the power to break strongholds
and bring deliverance.

January 13

JESUS DOES NOT FOLLOW US, WE FOLLOW HIM

Then Jesus said to his disciples,
"If any of you wants to be my follower,
you must give up your own way,
take up your cross, and follow me."
~ Matthew 16:24

Recently, I met a woman in prison. She spent her entire adult life in the clutches of sin. It took incarceration for her to repent and completely turn her life over to Jesus. I now consider this woman my friend. Every day, she touches lives, including mine, leaving a profound imprint of Christ.

She told me that since she'd heard that Jesus would be with us, he would follow her wherever she went and give her a "pass" on her depravity. She now understands that he is the Great Shepherd, we are his sheep, and we are to follow him. Following Jesus requires absolute obedience. He already knows what is best without ever having to consult with us.

Jesus will lead us to experiences we've never dreamed of. We will witness the great Jehovah-Rophe, who heals and mends our brokenness.

When we turn to Christ and repent, we receive the Holy Spirit and a new heart. We will glimpse the price that sin cost our Savior. We will see those who were spiritually blind encounter the joy of experiencing God for the first time. We will see lives that were broken made whole. Maybe you have stopped following Jesus, but now long to follow him again. It's never too late to run into his arms.

Jesus said, "You did not choose Me, but I chose you" (John 15:16).

Thank you, loving God, for choosing and forgiving me.
I cry out to you, my Father and God, "I need all of you."
Give me your peace as I cling to you.

January 14

THIS MORNING, HAVE YOU SEEN JESUS?

Jesus spoke to the people once more and said,
"I am the light of the world. If you follow me,
you won't have to walk in darkness,
because you will have the light that leads to life."
~ John 8:12

We don't know the topic for that particular morning as Jesus sat teaching in the temple—perhaps prayer, kindness, or maybe anxiety. Suddenly, a disheveled woman is dragged in and thrown down in front of everyone. I wonder if her accuser puffed out his chest as he declared, "Teacher, this woman was caught red-handed in the act of adultery. Moses, in the Law, gives orders to stone such persons. What do you say?" (John 3:3–6 MSG).

Jesus then bent down and wrote with his fingers in the dirt. Some scholars speculate that he might have written down all the sins of her confronters or the words "earth accuses earth." I often wonder why they didn't also bring the man caught in the act. Jesus must have expelled a heavy sigh as he responded to the crowd, "The sinless one among you, go first: Throw the stone" (John 8:6–8 MSG). He then bent down and continued writing on the ground.

From the oldest to the youngest, feet shuffled, eyes dropped, and stones could be heard dropping to the ground. The woman was left alone in front of her sinless King.

Jesus stood up and spoke, "Woman, where are they? Does no one condemn you?"

"No one, Master."

"Neither do I," said Jesus. "Go on your way. From now on, don't sin." (John 8:9–11 MSG).

From the mouth of Christ, thus our great assignment, to live our lives and sin no more.

Lord Jesus, help me go on my way and sin no more,
nor hypocritically judge others
caught in sin.

January 15

CAPTURE OUR REBELLIOUS THOUGHTS

We destroy every proud obstacle that keeps people
from knowing God. We capture their rebellious
thoughts and teach them to obey Christ.
~ 2 Corinthians 10:5

When our youngest grandson visited us as a toddler, he grew weary of all the different rules in our household compared to his home. Exasperated, he told us in a firm voice with his little arms crossed, "I'm not talking to anyone!"

At hearing the voice of a three-year-old defiantly declare his own verbal shutdown, I couldn't contain my laughter. My hysterical outburst only made the situation worse. After I calmed down, we hugged and had a sweet discussion.

Even as adults, we often let our thoughts dictate our words and moods in a way that echoes a child's frustration. I can't tell you how often I felt overwhelmed and snapped at my beloved family members, blaming my disposition on everything but my sin.

Scripture reminds us that we are soldiers and the battlefield is our mind. The thoughts we entertain can become our enemies. Our assignment is clear: protect our minds and refuse entrance to rebellious beliefs. God even tells us to take captive our "rebellious thoughts and teach them to obey Christ" (2 Corinthians 10:5). What if, every day, we boldly declared to these destructive thoughts, "Get out! You're not welcome here! My mind belongs to Christ!"

Imagine the transformation if we took this truth to heart daily, making it our mission to guard our minds as diligently as we guard our health.

Holy God, take charge of my mind.
Help me to capture every thought and
make it obedient to you.
Guide my words and deeds today,
that they may reflect
your love and truth.

January 16

DRINK DEEPLY

Why didn't you arrest me in the Temple?
I was there among you teaching every day.
But these things are happening to fulfill what
the Scriptures say about me.
~ Mark 14:49

Years ago, I experienced the deep pain that comes from betrayal by a trusted friend, followed by the sting of abandonment. Waves of depression swept over me, leaving me adrift in a sea of loneliness. It felt as if the weight of those emotions would never lift.

During that dark time, only the Word of God could comfort me. Every time I opened the Bible, it felt as though Jesus was holding me, breathing life back into my soul. Through Scripture, he reminded me that he, too, had suffered betrayal and desertion from those closest to him. He showed me that even in his deepest pain, my Savior Jesus turned to God's Word for strength and comfort. If he could, then so could I.

The Bible can console all of us in the same way. There will be moments when the actions of others leave us confused, or when events in life spiral into chaos. In these times, our faith and obedience to Christ are tested most. Immersing ourselves in the Word of God allows us to find the strength and clarity we need. If we build the habit of filling ourselves with his truth daily, we will already have a foundation to lean on when hardships come.

Let the Scriptures be your anchor, guiding and comforting you through every storm.

Help me, Lord, to drink deeply of your love and truth.
Fill my heart with a love worth giving,
and teach me to rely on your Word
for strength in every moment
of my life.

January 17

DON'T COMPARE YOURSELF TO OTHERS!

Oh, don't worry; we wouldn't dare say that we are as
wonderful as these other men
who tell you how important they are!
But they are only comparing themselves with each
other, using themselves as the standard of measurement.
How ignorant!
~ 2 Corinthians 10:12

When I was younger, I always compared myself to others. Other women were thinner, more beautiful, holier, and better mothers. I listened more to society's false expectations of who I should be, what I should look like, and how I should sound as a woman and mother. I was beyond weary. My focus was on man, not God.

Apparently, this has been an age-old battle with self, because Paul warned the Galatians not to compare themselves with others. Rather, they had to be concerned with their own responsibility before God.

Paul's warning to the Galatians pierced my heart and convicted me that I needed to be more focused on the eternal harvest and not the world.

Scripture reveals that God has a blueprint for every life and that if we live in constant fellowship with him, he will lead and direct us in fulfilling his plan. Many of us have been living for ourselves and not Jesus. If you have substituted the good for the best, do not despair. There is still time.

Wherever you are at this very moment, yield your life unconditionally to God and begin asking him, daily, for his best for your life. We cannot know the will of God unless we first come to the cross and confess our sinful nature.

Dear God, help me stop comparing myself to others
and only focus on the audience of One—
you, my eternal Father.

January 18

I HAVE SOME THINGS I NEED TO DO FIRST

The Spirit of the Sovereign LORD is upon me,
for the LORD has anointed me
to bring good news to the poor.
He has sent me to comfort the brokenhearted
and to proclaim that captives will be released
and prisoners will be freed.

~ Isaiah 61:1

I can't count the number of times I've told God, "I'll get right back to you when I have an extra minute." But each time I hear myself saying this, conviction quickly follows. I realize how insulting it is to put God on hold, as though his love, mercy, and protection aren't worthy of my immediate attention.

The truth is, that "extra minute" may never come. Time slips through our fingers, and opportunities to connect with our Creator can be lost forever.

Looking back over my life, I see countless moments when God's protection surrounded me. He clothed me in salvation and wrapped me in his goodness, even when I was too preoccupied to notice.

God's timing is always perfect. When he calls, we must respond in obedience without delay. Too often, we behave as if we have unlimited time to submit to him. But since tomorrow is never guaranteed, putting God first in our hearts and lives is essential.

Whenever we hear God's voice, our response is one of two things: faith or unbelief. We either obey or disobey. The choice is ours, but the consequences ripple far beyond the moment.

Precious Lord, forgive me for the times
I've put you on the back burner.
Teach me to walk in obedience
and to make you my priority.
May my heart always respond
to your call first.

January 19

ENCOUNTER THE LORD TODAY

His head and his hair were white like wool, as white as snow.
And his eyes were like flames of fire.
His feet were like polished bronze refined in a furnace,
and his voice thundered like mighty ocean waves.
~ Revelation 1:14–15

I've often heard people say, "If only I could have walked with Jesus, like the twelve disciples did, it would be so much easier to live as a Christian!" This common sentiment reveals a limited understanding of the Lord we serve.

Our culture often portrays Jesus as a gentle, passive leader—a figure strolling along the seashore, gathering children and forgiving sinners with a soft word. While these images reflect aspects of his ministry, they fall far short of capturing his full nature.

Father, Son, and Holy Spirit—our triune God—is an all-powerful, mighty, omniscient, omnipotent, and omnipresent Creator. To ignore or disobey God's Word is to forget the majesty and holiness of the

One we serve. When we elevate our fear of others above our reverence for God, we fail to grasp his greatness.

If you find yourself struggling with this, take a closer look at the powerful description of Jesus in Revelation. His blazing eyes, polished bronze feet, and thunderous voice remind us of the awesome God who dwells within our hearts. When we truly understand who he is, our perspective shifts. We move from seeking the fleeting approval of man to worshipping God.

Lord, may I encounter your mighty presence today.
Lift my eyes from the opinions of others
and draw my focus to you.
Fill me with your love and power,
and help me to live in awe
of your majesty.

January 20

COME AND RECEIVE

You learned about the Good News from Epaphras,
our beloved co-worker. He is Christ's faithful servant,
and he is helping us on your behalf.
He has told us about the love for others that
the Holy Spirit has given you.
~ Colossians 1:7–8

I always struggle with asking for help. Mired in my pride, I think I can do everything in my own strength. Eventually, by God's grace, things get better. Bills get paid. The dog comes home. The pantry is full. And the face we see in the morning mirror has a smile on it.

Then what?

I forget how bad things were and what God gave me. Sometimes I even think that God is lucky to have me on his side! Pride and self-righteousness can so easily cloud our view of our Creator. I guess we all struggle in this area.

Occasionally, we need an attitude or spiritual readjustment to remind us of the doctrine of salvation. We are saved solely because of God's grace. He has rescued and redeemed us!

To qualify for welfare, one must admit they're poor. To be admitted to a hospital, one must admit they're sick. And to go to heaven, one must admit they are a sinner and hell bound. That last truth can be a tough pill to swallow. It is difficult for a "decent" person to admit their shortcomings and lack of perfection. But we must to be saved.

Dear Jesus Christ, I thank you for the power that comes not
from what we know but whom we know.
Help us all come and
receive your grace
and help.

January 21

CHANGED THROUGH MEDITATION

Oh, the joys of those who do not follow the advice of the wicked,
or stand around with sinners, or join in with mockers.
But they delight in the law of the LORD,
meditating on it day and night.

~ Psalm 1:1–2

Several choices I made when I was younger led me down a dead-end and painful road. Still insisting on doing things my way, I pursued solving my problems by looking to the world instead of God. Thankfully, the Lord redirected my steps each time and brought me back to him.

Today, many people are searching for a more stable and peaceful life. The world falsely offers a myriad of paltry and temporary solutions to those who are filled with anxiety and unable to cope with their circumstances.

The Bible tells us that the only way to go through life securely is to walk in integrity (Proverbs 10:9) with God. Our eternal Father is our stability—a wealth of salvation, wisdom, and the source of all knowledge (see Isaiah 33:6). Without God, we are floundering in a meaningless existence.

What path are you on now? We all need to find our stability in Christ and follow the faithful road. God's rewards far supersede the benefits of the world.

Dear righteous Father, give me your stability.
Help me meditate and focus on you
as you alone provide, protect, and nourish
me every step of my journey.

January 22

LIFE DOES NOT END AT THE CEMETERY

Our days on earth are like grass;
like wildflowers,
we bloom and die.
~ Psalm 103:15

I will never forget that Sunday after church when we took our children to a local restaurant. In the foyer stood an enormous six-foot wooden dollhouse with glass doors. While at the table waiting for our food to arrive, our children asked if they could go and look at the dollhouse.

Of course I agreed. Our table had a perfect line of sight to our children. Then, within seconds, our four-year-old tried climbing up on the large platform to get a better view of inside the house, and the entire structure came crashing down on top of her. The large glass doors shattered everywhere.

Rushing toward the debris, we found our baby buried beneath the rubble, not moving. At that moment, my heart stopped. Miraculously, she only had a few minor cuts that did not require stitches. I'm convinced her guardian angel protected her.

The Bible reminds us that our days are like grass. For a moment, we flourish, but soon we wither and die. Yet the minutes of our lives can be flecked with the gold of eternity. Instead of wasting our lives that we so easily conform to, God exhorts us to redeem the time.

God made us different from other creatures. He made us, in his image, a living soul. One thousand years from this day, we will be more alive than we are at this very moment! Think about that. The Bible teaches that our lives do not end at the cemetery. There is a future life with God for those who trust his Son, Jesus Christ.

Father God, place an attitude of gratitude
in my heart every day.
In Jesus's name, I pray.

January 23

TIMES WHEN WE MUST TRUST

If you are faithful in little things,
you will be faithful in large ones.
But if you are dishonest in little things,
you won't be honest with greater responsibilities.
~ Luke 16:10

When I turned sixteen, my parents bought me a vehicle. Along with it came a set of rules for me to follow—all for my good. I had a curfew, and I knew that if I remained obedient, they would trust me more.

Likewise, God rewards those who are faithful. Throughout our lives, God is seeking to grow us in our faith in him. The Father will lead us into situations requiring "little" faith, and if we are among those who prove trustworthy, he will take us into situations that require even greater faith in him. Through each lesson, we receive the prize of trusting God at a higher level. As we advance in each step, our King will reveal himself more intimately to his faithful children.

The best way to know if we are prepared for a greater revelation of God is to test our level of obedience. Our righteous Father will bring us to our next assignment if we have been proven trustworthy—just like my parents did with my first car.

Every step of faith will lead us to a deeper understanding of our Lord. Thankfully, this invitation to know God more intimately is open to all believers through reading and meditating on Scripture.

Lord, teach us the power and blessings of obedience
and faithfulness to you.
Guide us to follow your living rules,
which are found in your Word,
the Holy Bible.

January 24
THAT CERTAIN HOPE

But blessed are those who trust in the Lord and
have made the Lord their hope and confidence.
~ Jeremiah 17:7

Today, we are accustomed to circumstances changing so
quickly. I know I can be so unnerved by breaking news. On
any given morning, we are bombarded by reports of another
school shooting, skyrocketing inflation, untreatable diseases, and new
street drugs readily available like candy. If the science of man and
humanity's protection of the world are the only sources of our hope,
we are in for a lot of trouble and heartache.

This echoes the lines from one of my favorite hymns: "My hope is
built on nothing less, than Jesus' blood and righteousness; I dare not
trust the sweetest frame, but wholly lean on Jesus' name. On Christ,
the solid Rock, I stand: all other ground is sinking sand."[1]

On what is your hope built? Is it that salary raise you've been
anticipating? Passing that end-of-school exam? Or maybe receiving

that specific electric scooter you have been dreaming about? Such dreams and desires are based on external elements over which we have little control. And all of these "hopes" pale in significance with the greatest of all—our hope of salvation found only in Jesus Christ.

Strengthen me, Lord, and help me not be drawn in by the world's standards, but by yours alone.

January 25
CHOICES

But when the young man heard this,
he went away sad,
for he had many possessions.
~ Matthew 19:22

As a teenager, I thought that if I could have more "things," I would be happy. Maybe you can relate? The rich young ruler in the verse above and I shared the same affliction in our youth. This young man was well-versed in the Word of God and professed his love for the Lord, but he loved his wealth more.

Isn't that just like us? I'm not necessarily referring to an overabundance in our bank account, the yacht awaiting us in the Caribbean, or the vacation home in the Swiss Alps. The "things" of the world can so easily be warped into a diversion from God. These can lead to sexual sin, greed, serving false gods such as drugs and alcohol, behavior that hurts others, using evil words when speaking, a bad temper, and lying lips.

Whenever the Lord speaks to us, we must adjust. This truth will dramatically affect our prayers and our lives. Now, I make a choice that each time I open my Bible, I need to disobey God or be prepared to *obey* what God tells me, including giving up the comforts of the world.

Thankfully, we are no longer under a death sentence. We can now rejoice! A new life, a new heart, and peace await us. Are you ready to choose God?

Dear God, help me to focus on your eternal fruit and
not the sin of the world. Watch me and help me
listen to your Word and make good choices.

January 26

WE CANNOT FIX OURSELVES

And the judgment is based on this fact:
God's light came into the world, but people loved the darkness more
than the light, for their actions were evil.

~ John 3:19

Growing up, I vividly remember my daddy saying, "Nothing good ever happens after midnight." And he'd continue, "All who do evil hate the light and will not come to the light, because it will show all the evil things they do" (John 3:20 NCV).

Of course, as a sixteen-year-old who knew almost everything, I chalked up his advice as old-fashioned. Smugly, I viewed him as the "only parent on earth who is this unbelievably strict" with their "almost-grown" daughter!

Now, of course, I would give anything to hear my daddy's wise counsel. I even hear myself repeating his words to my own now-grown children and grandchildren.

Thankfully, our Jesus *is* the Light of the world. Without God, we are cosmic rebels without a cause. We cannot fix ourselves in our own strength. Many of us have tried for years and figured out it doesn't work. Those of us who have let God do the repairs have seen victory.

There is good news. Jesus, our gracious Lord, has come to "fix us" and make us new. We can now experience true freedom at last! He has come to awaken us. We can now visualize, taste, and feel what real joy looks like. We can now live the life we have always longed for.

Dear Jesus, envelope me in your light—not the world's.
I know you are the only source of freedom for me.

January 27
CHANGED FROM WITHIN

This means that anyone who belongs to Christ
has become a new person.
The old life is gone; a new life has begun!
~ 2 Corinthians 5:17

I once asked a seasoned carpenter why he was tearing down a timeworn house instead of repairing it. He explained that it is better to use new materials than to repair the old. Also, it is usually more economical to construct a new house than to repair a dilapidated one.

I realized that this truth is even more true in the spiritual realm. The old nature, with its deceitfulness, depravity, and wickedness, must die and give way to a new nature, just like a tiny seed. Each of us is like a little acorn that needs to trust God and die to ourselves so that God can produce a giant oak tree from our lives.

God's Word declares, "I will give you a new heart and put a new spirit within you" (Ezekiel 36:26).

When I was in my teen years, this was a challenge. I still wanted to change my disposition in my own strength. No matter how much I tried, I couldn't. Being too prideful to admit that I needed God, I made things worse.

Now, of course, I see the good news: God can and does drastically change us for the better from within! If anyone is in Christ, they are a new creation. He doesn't want to patch us or paint over our damaged parts. He remakes us completely in his likeness.

Dear God, remake me better than I can even imagine.
Through you, I know I can change. I am a brand-new
creation in Christ. Change me from within.

January 28

ARE YOU STANDING OUTSIDE THE ARK?

It was by faith that Noah built a large boat to save his family
from the flood. He obeyed God, who warned him about
things that had never happened before.
By his faith Noah
condemned the rest of the world, and he received the
righteousness that comes by faith.

~ Hebrews 11:7

Can you imagine anything more heartbreaking than a man
who never quite decides it's time to hear from God?

I love it when God shows up unexpectedly. A few days ago, I
ran into a dear friend who I had not seen in almost twenty years. We
quickly recognized each other and started talking like we had just
spoken the night before. She shared with me the years of physical
ailments she had suffered all while trusting fully in God's healing
touch, and I stood in amazement at her infallible love, faith, and trust
in Jesus to bring her through life's storms.

God used Noah to warn the people, yet they laughed at him, mocked his words, and went about their own business. When the nonstop rains and floodwaters came for forty days and flooded the earth for one hundred and fifty days, every living thing outside the ark perished.

As believers, Jesus Christ is our Ark. Are you reconciled with God and saved from his wrath by the blood of Jesus? Our Savior welcomes all who admit their sins and declare him as their Lord. Are you in the Ark?

Dear God, save me and my loved ones from your wrath.
Help my unsaved family members run to you,
our Ark, and not perish in eternity.

January 29
THOSE UNGUARDED MOMENTS

Yes, I am the vine; you are the branches.
Those who remain in me, and I in them,
will produce much fruit.
For apart from me you can do nothing.
~ John 15:5

"When are you going to take care of that?" Irritation and sarcasm dripped from my voice as I pointed a finger at a task I had been asking my husband to take care of for weeks.

My husband, delicately balancing hundreds of things that were much more pressing than my request, ignored me.

Frustrated, I prayed to the Lord, telling on my husband like a child whose playmate stole their favorite toy. The Holy Spirit instantly convicted me of my impatience, sinful judgment, and lack of love for the man I adore, who has been a faithful, loving, and God-fearing husband for decades.

How we behave at home is the acid test for any Christian man or woman. It is easier to live an excellent life among our friends when we put our best foot forward and are conscious of public opinion than to act like Christ in our home. Our family sees us when our guard is down and exhaustion and stress fray our nerves. And they intimately know whether Christ lives in and through us.

How different would your home be if you consistently practiced these Christlike virtues?

Dear God, you are my Good Gardener.
Convict me during those unguarded moments when sin
arises and prune every branch
that is not producing.

January 30
WHAT DO OTHERS SEE IN YOU?

Always be full of joy in the Lord.
I say it again—
rejoice!
~ Philippians 4:4

Years ago, a beautiful woman sat in a pew several rows in front of us during church. Each week, she looked more miserable than the week before. Not knowing her or her situation, I prayed for her. After some time, her countenance convicted me that joy is one of the marks of a true believer. Christianity was never meant to make people miserable.

I felt God tug at my heart, and questions came to my mind:

Do I exude happiness as a Christian witness to the world?

Each day, does my life display the fruit of the Spirit?

Do I ooze "love, joy, peace, patience, kindness, goodness, faithfulness, gentleness, and self-control" (Galatians 5:22–23)?

Do others see the fruit of the Spirit in my life?

When our hearts are surrendered to the faith walk, we delight in seeing God use us in any way he pleases. When our plans and desires agree with our eternal Father and we accept his direction in our lives, our sense of joy, satisfaction, and fulfillment in life increases, no matter the circumstances.

Redeeming Lord, provide me with an attitude of
thanksgiving and a joyful expression to all
who could use a smile.
Help me exude the joy of Christ
each day.

January 31

DARK CORNERS IN YOUR LIFE

And forgive us our sins,
as we have forgiven those who sin against us.
~ Matthew 6:12

Many years ago, I needed to repent and ask someone to forgive me for my actions. I stewed, prayed, and argued with the Holy Spirit for far too long as he convicted me of my sin. Finally, I listened to God as he gently nudged me to repent.

Thankfully, the person I had sinned against graciously offered me forgiveness, and God miraculously knit our hearts together and strengthened our relationship. Few things are more precious to receive than forgiveness.

After carrying the burden of our sin, it is wonderfully freeing to know that the people we have wronged have forgiven us. In the Lord's Prayer, Jesus told his disciples to ask God for forgiveness every time they prayed. A day should not go by that we do not ask our Father to remove our sins.

If we are to be disciples, we must follow Jesus's teaching. If we withhold forgiveness from someone, our worship and prayers are futile (see Matthew 5:23–24). We need to ask God to make us aware of those dark corners in our lives where we are harboring bitterness and resentment.

Forgiving Father, teach me daily to live the prayer you
taught your disciples of old and make me
aware of the dark corners in life
that I need to repent from
and ask forgiveness for.

February

Romans 8:28

MJP

February 1

TO BE CONTENT IN ALL SEASONS

Not that I was ever in need,
for I have learned how to be content
with whatever I have.
~ Philippians 4:11

Throughout the years, as ranchers, we have had seasons of plenty and times of scarcity. During those lean times, peace can be distant. God, in his kindness, has always drawn close to me and comforted me no matter the condition of my heart or the numbers in our bank account.

True peace comes when we abandon our focus on the natural and what other people think, and focus on Christ. Popularity and praise can be far more dangerous for the Christian than persecution. They can turn us away from God without our even being aware of it, making us like those in Jesus's day who "loved the praise of men more than the praise of God" (John 12:43).

Our one consuming passion should be to please Christ. Then, whatever happens, we know he has permitted it to take place to teach us and to perfect us for his service.

As we prioritize our love for the Lord above all else, we stand in faith that we have the grace and strength to treat our neighbor with the same kindness we would want for ourselves.

Dear God, free me today from worrying about others'
opinions, and help me find satisfaction in whatever you,
my Father, decide as good.
Give me the grace to follow your commands, not the world's.
And help me walk in obedience, which is the greatest
form of worship.

February 2

THAT SAFE PLACE

God is our refuge and strength,
always ready to help in times of trouble.
~ Psalm 46:1

I can always tell when I've rushed or forgotten my special moments with my Lord each morning. The day slips by, and I feel empty inside like something is lacking. I can also be a tad bit cranky, as my fuse is shorter. Everything seems to irritate me. All because I missed the most important thing—my spiritual fuel for the day. Ever felt that way?

Time with God cannot be rushed or placed on the back burner. When we find ourselves in a hurry, our minds wander to the demands of the day instead of the greatness of God.

As all those demands begin pressing in on us, we need to push them back and refocus on God. He is our safe place and where we run to for strength. He alone comforts us when the world is trying to distract us.

Our eternal Father longs for our undivided attention and will use this quality time to bless us with his peace and presence. Besides, isn't he worth it?

Dear Jesus, help me always remember to carve out time
each day with you before anything else.
You are my Savior and my priority,
as time spent with you is
the wisest investment.

February 3

SEEKING GOD DURING OUR DARKEST MOMENTS

And it is impossible to please God without faith.
Anyone who wants to come to him must believe that God
exists and that he rewards those who sincerely seek him.
~ Hebrews 11:6

Our faith largely determines our relationship with God. Throughout my walk with the Lord, I have had difficult seasons, such as the death of our daughter, when trusting my Father was the hardest thing imaginable. I blamed my Creator and became unbelievably sad.

Getting up each day took an extraordinary amount of effort and faith. The last thing I wanted to do was trust the God who took our darling Carmen home too early. It took time for me to seek the Lord. My Father then softened my heart by reminding me he knows what is best for dear Carmen, who now is celebrating with Jesus in heaven.

God always responds to us when we earnestly seek him, even though he might not provide the answers we want. When we say, "I love God but have difficulty trusting him," it's understandable that we may not feel completely at ease. It isn't easy to love someone or something we don't trust.

Faith does not eliminate problems. Faith keeps us in a trusting relationship amid our problems. Some may say, "I'm not much of a person of faith. I'm more of a practical person." You will never do anything more practical than placing your trust in the Lord, especially when life is the darkest.

Father of the universe, keep me seeking you, especially
during the darkest moments in my life.
Give me the strength and joy
to keep trusting and obeying you
despite the circumstances.

February 4

CHANGING CLOTHES VS. CHANGING YOUR MIND

Jesus replied,
"I tell you the truth,
unless you are born again,
you cannot see the Kingdom of God."
~ John 3:3

Unfortunately, changing clothes doesn't change the person. Outward discipline doesn't alter what is within. And new habits don't make a new soul.

Jesus coined the phrase "born again." He first used it when talking to Nicodemus, who was, by the world's standards, a good man. He was a Pharisee, a religious ruler. He had been taught, like everyone else during that time, that if you change the outside, you change the inside. He had very little knowledge of how only God can change people.

This concept of being "born again" was new to Nicodemus, and he questioned Christ, "How can someone be born when they are old?"

and declared, "Surely they cannot enter a second time into their mother's womb to be born!" (John 3:4 NIV).

"You are Israel's teacher," said Jesus, "and do you not understand these things? Very truly I tell you, we speak of what we know, and we testify to what we have seen, but still you people do not accept our testimony" (John 3:10–11 NIV)

Dare I say, I am always astonished when God heals a body. It is extraordinary that God hears our prayers. He gives us new eyes so we can see by faith, a new mind so we can have the mind of Christ. Are you reborn as a new creation in Christ?

Gracious and forgiving Father,
again I ask with a grateful heart to be reborn.
Wash me clean with your
Holy Spirit.

February 5
NO REGRETS

That is why I am suffering here in prison.
But I am not ashamed of it, for I know the one in whom I trust, and I
am sure that he is able to guard what I have
entrusted to him until the day of his return.
~ 2 Timothy 1:12

Does Christianity work? Does anything really happen when a person repents of their sins and receives Christ by faith through grace?

One great hero of faith had exactly that happen to him. Billy Graham, raised on a dairy farm in North Carolina during the Great Depression, did not experience the advantages most young people enjoy today. Even though he grew up in a Christian home, at fifteen he preferred baseball to religion and wanted nothing to do with God, the Bible, and the church.[1]

But one strange and God-orchestrated night, an unexpected event happened. A friend persuaded Billy to go to a Mordecai Hamm revival meeting. Billy kept going back, and one night he accepted the invitation to commit his life to Christ. At that very moment, the Savior gave Billy a whole new direction for this life.

Family, friends, and neighbors saw a difference in the young Billy Graham. His grades at school picked up. His attitude toward others changed, and he began to seek the Lord's will instead of his own. He stated that he did not become perfect, but God was changing him, making him more like Christ each day.

From the words of a man who led many a lost soul to Christ, "I have never met anyone who regretted giving his life to Christ. And neither will you."[2]

Dear God, I grant you permission to guide
and direct my life so that I may be
instrumental in leading
lost souls toward you.

February 6

COME WITH A BOLDNESS

Keep on asking, and you will receive what you ask for.
Keep on seeking, and you will find.
Keep on knocking, and the door will be opened to you.
~ Matthew 7:7

Our grands are not the least bit bashful about asking for things from us. As grandparents, we are easy targets for those beautiful brown eyes and soft, childlike voices that implore us at every toy store, "Doodle, can I have one of these, pleeeassseee?"

Kids must come with an internal sucker detector, and as grandparents we must have a bullseye on our backs. Children would not be typical if they did not brazenly make their needs known and ask for everything.

I imagine God is the same way with us. Our eternal Father is so pleased when we, as his children, bring our burdens to him. He even tells us to "make your requests known" (Philippians 4:6 NASB). And he encourages us, his children, to "come boldly to the throne of our gracious God. There we will receive his mercy, and we will find grace to help us when we need it most" (Hebrews 4:16).

I find that to be true, especially if I spend a sleepless night worrying, as I have been known to do. When I get up with my Bible in hand and find a quiet place to sit, my heart is instantly quieted. What is troubling you today? Is your heart burdened because of some problem that threatens to overcome you? Are you filled with anxiety and worry? Go to the Lord.

Dear Lord, I am grateful for your invitation to come boldly
to your throne, make my requests known to you,
and cast all my worries and concerns upon you.
Calm my restless spirit and
bring me peace.

February 7

WHAT DOES YOUR HEART REVEAL?

Remember how the LORD your God led you through the
wilderness for these forty years, humbling you and testing
you to prove your character, and to find out whether or not
you would obey his commands.

~ Deuteronomy 8:2

I believe I suffered from common sense amnesia during my early
twenties. I seemed to forget everything I learned, as now I
thought I "knew" everything! Thankfully, older and wiser
Christians and family members came alongside me, leading me back
to Christ. Times of rebellion or questioning our faith are common.
Some of the staunchest Christians I know have confessed to periods in
their lives when they mistrusted the Bible, Jesus Christ, and God.

God's Word declares, "The heart is deceitful above all things"
(Jeremiah 17:9 NIV). Unfortunately, it doesn't take much for us to sin
and accept unbelief as faith. A philosopher once stated, "A little

knowledge leads men away from Christianity, but a great deal brings them back to it."[1]

Perhaps God is testing you and your faith today. Have you become bitter toward God because of where he, in his goodness, has led you? Or are you called to trust your eternal Father more as a result of what you have gone through?

Father God,
I ask that you mold and change my heart
into a model that trusts you more.
I pray my unwavering faith would
be an example to others.
I pray that my family and I would know you
and follow the one and
only true God.

February 8

GOD HAS PLACED YOU AS A WATCHMAN

I will climb up to my watchtower and stand at my guardpost.
There I will wait to see what the LORD says
and how he will answer my complaint.
~ Habakkuk 2:1

My mother always instilled in me that my most important jobs as a mother were to equip my children to leave our proverbial nest and start their own homes, and to pray for them each day. I have taken her advice and am amazed at how freeing it is to empower my children to live independently. My fears for them have blossomed into trust in God for them and their safety.

Even now, as my children have children of their own, I still stand as their watchman. God continues to forward me spiritual alerts on specific dangers they are facing. I realize now as I fall down on my knees in prayer at my guard post, my job is vital.

As a Christian, you have been placed as a watchman by God—for yourself, your friends, your family, and your church. It is critical that you be attentive to what God is saying so you can be alerted to and pray for what is coming. Maybe it is a friend in crisis (who you didn't even know about) who needs a nugget of truth from God's Word. Or, as your family faces difficult challenges, maybe God will speak to you on how to pray and reveal how you can help them.

My all-seeing God, may I strive to be more attentive to every word and warning
that comes from you.
Continue to use me to pray and
intercede for my loved ones.

February 9

YOU WILL NEVER FACE A SHORTFALL

And God will generously provide all you need.
Then you will always have everything you need and
plenty left over to share with others.
~ 2 Corinthians 9:8

Not so long ago, I felt led to start a discipleship class in our church for people after baptism. When I presented the idea to my pastor, he thought it was a good plan and encouraged me to move forward.

I was thrilled yet confused about my next steps, but the Lord assured me he would never leave me or forsake me. I felt him at my side during those Sunday afternoon sessions. And I understood that for every good work I attempt, I would never face a shortfall of God's grace to successfully complete the task I had been given. What my Savior did for me, he will do for you, too.

When God asks you to do something, do you relate to him as the abundant Provider? Do you remember that God never does anything halfway? I can so easily forget this about him.

God reminded me that this is true regarding his grace. When we seek to perform a good work that he has asked us to do, we will always find an ample supply of his grace to sustain us. And when we begin to grow weary and lose heart in the work we are doing, God's grace will uphold us. He gives us his love for his people, so we continue.

Sovereign Lord, may I take heart this day while trusting you,
when asking what I can do for you,
that I may complete the task successfully,
remembering you supply more
than enough to complete each task.

February 10
WHY ARE YOU FEARFUL, YOU OF LITTLE FAITH?

The disciples went and woke him up, shouting,
"Lord, save us! We're going to drown!"
Jesus responded, "Why are you afraid?
You have so little faith!"
Then he got up and rebuked the wind and waves, and
suddenly there was a great calm.
~ Matthew 8:25–26

Sometimes the storms of life surround us without warning. Even if we have notice, the intensity can be quite terrifying. Our area has been experiencing ferocious wildfires, scorching over one million acres of once beautiful towns, ranches, and cattle. The devastating aftermath is absolutely heartbreaking, especially since this is so close to our home and has affected so many Texans we know and love.

Knowing that the Lord already knows our weaknesses, I often questioned Jesus's rebuke of Peter, "Why are you afraid? You have so little faith!" when their boat was about to capsize in a sudden, violent storm on the Sea of Galilee. I also would have been terrified and called out, "Lord, save us!"

Faith in God's mighty power is released into the life of a Christian. Unfortunately, this level of faith is only activated in believers' lives through our storms.

If our prayer life is infiltrated with anxieties, we have denied ourselves the greatest single power that God has made available to us. Without a deep understanding of God, it is impossible for us to stand during our storms. God wants to build our understanding of him until our faith is sufficient to trust and obey him in each situation. Jesus knew that the redemption of the world rested on his disciples believing in him. Friend, that rebuke and encouragement is also for you and me.

Father God, make me ready and willing to go out into the
world to be your representative.
Help me have the faith to
trust you in my storms.

February 11

WHEN CHRIST CALLS US FOR A SPECIFIC TASK

So Jesus sent two of them into Jerusalem with
these instructions: "As you go into the city, a man carrying a
pitcher of water will meet you. Follow him."
~ Mark 14:13

When I was in college, I felt a sudden, overwhelming nudge to visit a friend I hadn't spoken to in months. I had no idea why, but the thought wouldn't leave me. When I finally knocked on her door, she broke down in tears and shared that she had been praying for someone to come because she felt completely alone. That moment taught me the importance of obeying God's prompting, even when I didn't understand the reason.

The two disciples in the verse above were given very detailed instructions to go to a certain town and look for a particular man performing a specific task. The men obeyed and found everything just as Jesus had said.

Obedience to Christ's commands always brings fulfillment. God tells us to obey his commands quickly (Psalm 119:32). When the Lord gives us instructions, we need to obey immediately. Waiting until we have figured it all out and everything makes perfect sense in the natural is disobedience. Many times, God will lead us to do things that we will not fully understand until after we've done them. He does not usually reveal all the details of his will when he first speaks to us. Instead, he plants a thought and waits for our reliance upon him. That is how we build our faith in God and is known as the "faith walk."

If there is any directive God has given you and you chose to ignore it, repent and *obey* that directive immediately. Then watch God's perfect plan unfold in your life.

Faithful God, may I always be willing to listen
for your voice and heed your instruction.
Help me obey your commands
immediately.

February 12

WHEN ALL ELSE FAILS, PRAY

Devote yourselves to prayer with
an alert mind and a thankful heart.
~ Colossians 4:2

The most wonderful part of my day is waking up to the aroma of coffee. After I get out of bed with my Bible in hand, I can't wait to sit in my favorite chair. I snuggle in with my warm throw wrapped around me and sip a steaming cup of coffee with the sweet fragrance of the Word of God, and my heart is awakened. This special quiet time with God is where I lay all my requests at his feet and get filled up to fight my battles. My conversations with my Father each morning over my mug of java begin a beautiful day for me. I need to get plugged into my source before I start my day.

Too few of us have learned how to access the power in the Scriptures through prayer. Those who have a personal relationship with the living God have already discovered this secret. All the answers to our problems can come through communication with our eternal Father.

Prayer is vital; it's the only way God can change the human heart. A person can be more powerful on his or her knees than behind the most formidable weapons ever developed by man. This is absolutely the greatest privilege on this side of heaven.

Seeking God first through prayer should be our first line of defense each and every day, especially when we view a situation as helpless.

Our great and holy Father,
I pray that I may be an example to those
I love most in this life.
Help me always remember to start my day in your Word,
praying for those I love and
for those you place on my heart.

February 13

LOOKING FOR LOVE IN ALL THE WRONG PLACES

Instead,
be kind to each other, tenderhearted,
forgiving one another, just as God through
Christ has forgiven you.
~ Ephesians 4:32

Lately, I've been forced to think of several people in my life whom I've found less than easy to be around. It seems like no matter what happens, we aren't getting along. I realized that I haven't been as forgiving, kind, and tenderhearted to them as God has been to me.

Praying, I felt the Lord shine a bright light of questions on my soul. How well do I love the people in my life? Does the way I treat people reflect the way God has treated me? Conviction set in. I had to dig deep to think about these questions before answering, and finally came to the realization I probably needed to take inventory of my heart and repent once again.

This is serious business because God is the CEO of our lives and is watching closely. It takes a lot of grace to love those who have been a source of heartache, abuse, rejection, or loneliness.

I ask you, if conventional wisdom says that a lack of love implies a lack of effort, do we need to try harder, dig deeper, and strain more? Or could it be more than that? Have we skipped an essential step? Are we trying to give what we don't have? In the body of Christ, we are commissioned to accept one another in love. Should I decide to disobey Jesus by not loving another this time around, then I need an attitude adjustment.

There is only one relationship that we get to receive such constant love that never fails, and that's our relationship with our Savior.

Loving God,
I ask for the heart of Christ,
that I may love others
just as you have loved.

February 14

DON'T KEEP A LIST OF WRONGS

It does not demand its own way.
It is not irritable, and
it keeps no record of being wronged.
~ 1 Corinthians 13:5

My husband and I are always amazed at how crazy everyone becomes preparing for a day about love. Flowers, balloons, and chocolates are in every storefront. It's the busiest time to go out and enjoy a good meal, as the lines are so long and the wait staff are so harried.

Long ago, we decided that we need to be the love of Christ every day. It's so easy to make a list of wrongs. We all know that friends aren't always friendly, neighbors aren't always neighborly, and some coworkers simply don't work out. Even superiors can sometimes feel more bossy than supportive.

God is calling us to hand over our list of wrongs. He asks us to take those hurts, betrayals, and disappointments and lay them at the foot of the cross—once and for all. We can't go back for them. We need his love to heal what bitterness destroys.

Paul offers us this life-changing perspective: "If someone does wrong to you, forgive that person because the Lord forgave you" (Colossians 3:13). Forgiveness isn't just a gift we give others; it's freedom for our own souls. When we forgive, we release the weight of resentment and make room for God's peace to fill our hearts.

So today, let's give God our anxieties before they take root and inhibit us. Hand him your list of wrongs and trust him to heal the wounds they left behind. Choose the love of Christ.

Lord Jesus, thank you for the forgiveness you freely give.
You openly embrace, lift up, and protect me.
Help me to extend that same grace to others
and release the burdens of sin
that I should never carry.

February 15

A SERVANT LIKE JESUS

For I want you to understand what really matters,
so that you may live pure and blameless lives until the day of
Christ's return. May you always be filled with the fruit of
your salvation—the righteous character produced in your life
by Jesus Christ—for this will bring
much glory and praise to God.
~ Philippians 1:10–11

I once volunteered at an event that required hours of physical labor—setting up tables, unloading heavy supplies, and cleaning up afterward. I signed up with excitement, but as exhaustion set in, I found myself questioning why I had agreed to do all of this in the first place.

In the midst of my grumbling thoughts, an elderly volunteer beside me smiled and said, "We're serving others just as Jesus served us." Her simple statement reshaped my perspective, reminding me of the ultimate Servant we strive to emulate.

Jesus is the ultimate example of servanthood and selflessness. He deliberately stripped himself of everything—his divine rights and privileges—and crossed the unthinkable chasm between God and man. The unlimited God became personified into the confines of a limited man. Thankfully, Jesus Christ remained in his divinity through it all.

And from the human viewpoint, Jesus descended to the lowest point possible. But then he took one more step, the deepest descent of all: the cross. He became sin for us. This act of humility changed the trajectory for all humanity.

What has God asked you to do, as his servant, that you are struggling with?

Lord Jesus, you are truly our ultimate example of
selflessness. May we set our eyes on your divine rights
and privileges, none of which we contributed to,
to express our total gratitude.

February 16

PEW-WARMING IS NO LONGER AN OPTION

I will bring that group through the fire and make them pure.
I will refine them like silver and purify them like gold.
They will call on my name, and I will answer them.
I will say, "These are my people," and they will say,
"The LORD is our God."
~ Zechariah 13:9

Sitting in the pew one Sunday morning, I realized I was merely going through the motions. My mind drifted, my heart felt uninspired, and my worship was hollow. I realized that I had let the cares of life eclipse God. It wasn't until I served on a ministry team that I felt that spark. Serving others rekindled my passion and transformed my understanding of what it meant to truly follow Christ.

Who is the King of glory? The Lord our God? The emperor of Judah? The soaring eagle of eternity? The noble admiral of the kingdom?

Jesus is not your run-of-the-mill Messiah. His story is extraordinary. All God and all man, he allowed a minimum-wage Roman soldier to drive a nail into his wrist. He demanded purity yet stood for the rights of a repentant adulterer. Let's follow his sandal print and sit on the cold, hard floor of the cave where he was born. Watch and inhale his divinity as he touched and healed the sores of the unclean. Smile along with him as he showed compassion to the woman at the well and the foolish Jewish scribes and leaders.

Seeing Jesus changes people. Fake religion will no longer suffice. Pew-warming is no longer an option. Once you have experienced him, you will be forever changed.

God of the universe, may my heart always be open to you
and your Son, my Savior Jesus Christ.
May I always follow you unto
the ends of the earth.

February 17

JESUS DID NOT INCLUDE AN EXCEPTION CLAUSE

Leave your sacrifice there at the altar.
Go and be reconciled to that person.
Then come and offer your sacrifice to God.
~ Matthew 5:24

I
f there is ever a Scripture that is constantly disobeyed, it is this mandate to be reconciled. God's Word does not tell us to try to be reconciled, but clearly tells us to do it.

I don't know about you, but for me that command from our Savior is harder to obey than others. Maybe you have responded like I have so many times before: "God, you don't know how bad they hurt me! It's unreasonable to ask me to take the initiative to restore our relationship."

Unfortunately, Jesus did not include an exception clause for our reconciliation. If the person is an enemy, Jesus said to love them and to pray for those who persecute us (Matthew 5:44).

But what happens when the other party is unwilling or it's not wise or safe to reconcile? Our job is to continue to obey God's Word and "do all that you can to live in peace with everyone" (Romans 12:18). Forgiveness needs to be in our heart first.

On the contrary, the world preaches, "Assert yourself. Get even."

Jesus says, "Deny yourself. Show unconditional love." We can obey this command through grace, mercy, and forgiveness shown to us through our Savior's ultimate sacrifice for us on the cross.

Is there someone with whom you need to make peace?

Merciful God, where reconciliation is needed, may I
immediately obey you as an act of praise,
and worship you instead of giving in to sin and
unforgiveness.
Help me quickly forgive and
be reconciled with those
who have hurt me.

February 18

KEEP YOUR EYES FIXED ON HEAVEN

You suffered along with those who were thrown into jail, and
when all you owned was taken from you, you accepted it
with joy. You knew there were better things waiting
for you that will last forever.
~ Hebrews 10:34

Years ago, I was far from home and traveling alone for an
extended period. After weeks of unfamiliar faces and
surroundings, I felt a deep sense of homesickness. But then,
unexpectedly, I bumped into an old friend in the most unlikely place.
That one familiar face brought immediate comfort and joy. I imagine
heaven will feel like that—only magnified beyond anything we've ever
experienced.

Some people think heaven will be dull and boring, but nothing could
be further from the truth. Our Father's house will be a beautiful and
happy home where there will be work to be done. John wrote, "His

servants shall serve him" (Revelation 22:3). Each one of us will be given the task that suits our individual powers, tastes, and abilities.

Our heavenly home will be filled with family and friends. Have you ever been homesick in a strange place and then experienced the joy of seeing a familiar face? Not one of us who enters the Father's house will feel lonely or strange, for we who have put our trust in Christ are part of his family.

I often think about the moment when we will meet our heavenly Father face-to-face. Can you imagine the instant feeling of love and belonging, the sense that we are truly home? It's a reunion like no other—a long-awaited homecoming that will last for eternity.

Father God, may I keep my eyes fixed on heaven.
I know the welcome mat has my name on it—
for I'm a child of God and
I can't wait to come home!

February 19

TEN MINUTES A DAY

Then you will have healing for your body
and strength for your bones.
~ Proverbs 3:8

At this time of year, do you find your energy running low? Everyone says to keep going when life gets tough. Easier said than done! Rest assured, you are not alone.

Looking back over my journals from years past, I notice the same feelings of weariness this time every year. Tiredness can prevent effective and successful living.

Once, a dear friend shared her physical exhaustion due to a lack of energy and not sleeping well. I told her I had recently experienced the same thing and had to remind myself that God is the giver of life, energy, and a peaceful night's sleep! I have found that there is no better way to replenish my energy levels than to spend ten minutes every morning spiritually getting closer and closer to the Lord. The renewal of body, mind, and spirit only comes from our Father. After all, he created our energy in the first place. Once I readjusted my schedule to incorporate spending time with God by sitting quietly with my eyes closed and meditating on him, I received the much-needed overfilling by the Holy Spirit.

Creator of everything, help me to adjust my schedule to
spend time with you,
who provides everything,
including my energy every morning
and my sleep each night.

February 20

IN THE WORLD BUT NOT OF THE WORLD

Those people belong to this world, so they speak from the
world's viewpoint, and the world listens to them.
But we belong to God, and those who know God listen to us.
If they do not belong to God, they do not listen to us.
That is how we know if someone has the Spirit of truth
or the spirit of deception.

~ 1 John 4:5–6

Years ago, I was at an event where I found myself surrounded
by people with values and lifestyles vastly different from my
own. The conversations, humor, and attitudes were heavily
influenced by a worldly perspective, and I felt out of place. But instead
of retreating, I engaged, sharing glimpses of my faith when the
opportunity arose. By the end of the event, someone privately thanked
me for bringing a refreshing perspective.

As believers, we need to be like the Gulf Stream waters—be in the
world yet not absorbed by it. The Gulf Stream is a strong ocean
current that brings warm water from the Gulf of Mexico into the

Atlantic Ocean. It maintains its warm temperature as it travels into the icy waters of the North Atlantic.

If we are to fulfill our purpose in this world, we must not be chilled by the indifferent, godless society and environment we inhabit.

Romans 12:2 says, "Do not be conformed to this world." It is true that Jesus surrounded himself and dined with sinners, but he did not allow their views to overwhelm him and change him to their ways. Like the Gulf Stream, Jesus changed those around him to be more like him instead of the world. Our social interactions should be opportunities to share our faith with those who do not yet know Christ.

God of creation, may I challenge myself to make a point to
go out into all the world and not be conformed by it,
but to be a light and make more of your disciples.

February 21
PRAYERS OF HIS CHILDREN

I tell you, you can pray for anything,
and if you believe that you've received it,
it will be yours.
~ Mark 11:24

Before our prayers can mean anything to God, they must first mean something to us. I remember a night when I listened to my young daughter say her bedtime prayer. With hands clasped and eyes tightly shut, she whispered, "Dear God, please take care of Mommy, Daddy, and my sister, and make sure our puppy has sweet dreams."

It was simple but heartfelt. In that moment, I realized the profound difference between rote prayers and genuine, heartfelt communication with God.

Mindlessly repeating prayers we memorized as children, such as "Now I lay me down to sleep," or offering vague requests like "Bless everyone everywhere," doesn't reflect the depth of true prayer. Prayer is meant to be a sincere conversation with God where we bring him our deepest worries and joys. God delights in these authentic prayers from his children, no matter their age. This morning, a friend shared with me how her grandson's earnest bedtime prayer brought her renewed inspiration and encouragement.

Let us not pray casually, but come boldly before the throne of grace, trusting that we will find mercy and grace in our time of need. The unguarded, genuine prayers of children remind us all of the importance of praying with sincere hearts.

Loving God, guide me daily, by your Holy Spirit,
to come before your throne as a repentant sinner.
Hear my heartfelt prayer,
merciful Father.

February 22

AN ENHANCED SUNDAY SCHOOL LESSON

You have seen what I did to the Egyptians.
You know how I carried you on eagles' wings
and brought you to myself.
~ Exodus 19:4

"Why do all great stories of miraculous answers to prayer come from remote African villages or war-torn cities in Ukraine?"

"Why does it appear that God is only visibly active on the mission fields?"

"Why don't we get to see miracles?"

The middle school students peppered their Sunday School teacher with these questions as I looked in from the hallway.

The teacher at the front of the room smiled. "Why do you think?"

Silence.

Until one student offered, "Maybe that's all they have, faith in God. Everything else failed them."

I smiled and continued my walk down the church corridor. I agreed.

I believe God is most active when we are reaching out. The Creator of the universe stretches out when we look up. When we stop trying to run our lives on our strength, we get to witness Jehovah's power.

Do you have the faith for a miracle? Are you reaching out to the Creator of the universe?

Dear God, give me faith for miracles.
Help me always reach out to you.
Lift me up on eagles' wings
like you did the Israelites when
you brought them out of Egypt.
Allow me to witness your
incredible power.

February 23
TUNE IN TO GOD

This message was kept secret
for centuries and generations past,
but now it has been revealed to God's people.
~ Colossians 1:26

A re we tuned in to God? Does he still speak to us? Is he trying to reach us?

What if the problem is not with God but with us?

This reminds me of long family road trips in the car when I was a child. We didn't have iPads, phones, laptops, or movies. We didn't even have a Walkman to play cassette tapes. We only had one radio, which Dad controlled the entire way from Texas to Colorado!

Once we started driving through the mountain passes, the reception went from partially clear to total static. From time to time, I've found comfort in the white noise from static. Just like today, when I become more focused on the mind-numbing white noise from the world instead of tuning into my heavenly Father.

We can know God only in one way: what he has revealed to us through his Word, the Holy Bible, where he spoke to the authors through the inspiration of the Holy Spirit. The fingerprints of our Father are also evident in the world he created, the birth of a newborn, and the end of life in the world of one of his faithful servants as they transition into eternity with him.

God is trying to break through the noise to us, but we must be willing to tune in to his Word. Are we still enough to hear him?

Father, ignite a fresh passion in my heart for only you.
Help me block out the noise
and focus only on you
and your Word.

February 24

HIS PERFECT PLAN

Don't copy the behavior and customs of this world,
but let God transform you into a new person by
changing the way you think.
Then you will learn to know God's will for you,
which is good and pleasing and perfect.
~ Romans 12:2

Have you ever tried to make a big decision with only a small part of the picture? Would you buy a house after seeing only the laundry room? Or purchase a car by only glancing at the taillights online? What about recommending a book after reading just one paragraph?

Of course not. That wouldn't make any sense. Good decisions require a clear, full picture, and that's true not only when buying a house, buying a car, or choosing a book, but also in how we view life.

It's easy to judge someone based on their lowest moments, but one mistake doesn't define a person. Likewise, one success doesn't make someone perfect. We're all a work in progress, shaped and transformed by God if we're willing to trust him with our life.

What challenges are you facing right now? What sins are tempting you? Instead of letting them define you, allow God to rewrite your story into a testimony of his grace and love.

Remember, God has already written the conclusion of our journeys, and our Father's plan for us is good, pleasing, and perfect.

Lord, transform my mind and heart.
Help me to trust your plan even
when I can't see the whole picture.
Lead me to follow your will and
find peace in your perfect
conclusion for my life.

February 25

FINAL INSTRUCTION

Show them great respect and wholehearted love
because of their work. And live peacefully with each other.
Brothers and sisters, we urge you to warn those who are
lazy. Encourage those who are timid. Take tender care of those who
are weak. Be patient with everyone.
~ 1 Thessalonians 5:13–14

Over the years, there have been moments in my life when I would close my eyes and try to listen—hoping to hear my daughter's voice just one more time. What are the "one-more-times" in your life?

The disciple John found himself stranded on the Island of Patmos, surrounded by the sea and far from those he loved. He longed to hear God's voice once again, to be reminded of the hope and assurance Jesus had spoken. Even in his isolation, John kept his eyes and ears focused on God's promises, dreaming of the day he would hear the Lord's voice again.

In this world we face challenges, losses, and moments of loneliness. But for those who live for God's eternal kingdom, there is hope. When life's waves toss us into uncertainty, we can remember his promises: those who endure will be saved. Thankfully, that promise also declares that the gospel will reach every corner of the earth, and the end will come.

How will you use your "one-more-times"? Spend them on what truly matters—being with those you love, building relationships that reflect God's love and honor him.

Eternal Father, help me to use the time and resources
I have left to invest in what matters most—
relationships that bring you glory.
May I set aside the unnecessary
and focus on what lasts
forever.

February 26
WORLDLY PROPAGANDA

You must have the same attitude
that Christ Jesus had.
~ Philippians 2:5

I once attended a family gathering where the television was playing in the background. A commercial came on that glorified indulgence and self-centered living, with the tagline "You deserve it all." It was catchy and well-produced, but it left me unsettled.

As I watched, my young niece turned and asked, "Do we really need everything they show?" Her innocent question struck me. Even a child could sense the hollowness of the world's constant push for more.

Our unguarded minds can easily become battlefields, constantly influenced by worldly propaganda. Whether we realize it or not, we're bombarded by messages urging us to focus on ourselves—our desires, our wants, our pleasures. These worldly voices try to push God aside, convincing us that other things are more important.

Yet, amid all the noise, God's voice still calls to us, "Do not be conformed to this world, but be transformed by the renewing of your mind" (Romans 12:2 NIV). We're reminded that we don't have to live for ourselves but can live for our King and follow his will, which is good, acceptable, and perfect.

Here's a challenge: Next time you open your Bible or spend time in prayer, take note of how much time you dedicate to God. Compare it to the time spent on screens, entertainment, or social media. Is God truly getting the attention he deserves in your life?

Lord of the universe, remove the distractions that clutter my mind.
Renew my thoughts so they are centered
on what truly matters—
your will and your Word.

February 27

ARE YOU BEING MADE PERFECT?

Even though Jesus was God's Son, he learned obedience
from the things he suffered. In this way,
God qualified him as a perfect High Priest,
and he became the source of eternal salvation
for all those who obey him.
~ Hebrews 5:8–9

D o you remember the 1972 song "Why Me" by Kris Kristofferson? It was created during one of the darkest times in his life, yet it became a massive hit. There's a reason why stories like his resonate—because there's something redemptive about suffering.

When we lost our daughter, those were the darkest days I had ever experienced. Looking back, I realize that they were also the richest times during my faith walk. God divinely comforted and molded me. Stripped of my reliance, I was forced to lean fully on him. In the midst of suffering, I discovered a deeper faith that I never thought possible.

We all endure difficulties to some degree, but the good news is that through the most challenging times in our lives, we can become like Jesus. There are some things that God can build into your life only through suffering. Even Jesus, the sinless Son of God, endured extraordinary amounts of torture and agony. It was through his suffering that he became our perfect High Priest, the Savior who offers eternal salvation to all who follow him.

If we allow bitterness to take root in our hearts during hardships, we block off parts of our lives from God's work. It's in surrendering even our pain that we find completeness in him.

Faithful Father, keep my heart from growing bitter
when I face suffering. Teach me to learn obedience
and trust in you, even when it's hard.
Help me to embrace
the process of being made
complete in you.

February 28

ARE YOU FIRMLY PLANTED?

Oh, the joys of those who do not follow the advice of the
wicked, or stand around with sinners, or join in with
mockers. But they delight in the law of the LORD,
meditating on it day and night.
~ Psalm 1:1–2

A few years ago, I planted a small tree in my backyard. At first
it seemed fragile, bending under the weight of heavy rain
and strong winds. I worried it wouldn't survive. But over
time, its roots grew deeper, anchoring it firmly in the soil. Now, no
matter the storm, it stands tall, its branches reaching toward the sky.
Watching that tree thrive reminds me of the importance of being
firmly rooted—in Christ.

What does it mean to be firmly planted in Christ? In a world that is
constantly shifting, it's easy to be swept away by popular opinions,
fleeting trends, and the voices of those who do not follow God. We are
called to delight in the law of the Lord—to meditate on it day and
night. This means more than just reading a few verses now and then;

it involves immersing ourselves in God's truth, allowing his Word to saturate our thoughts, direct our actions, and guide our choices.

When we are firmly planted in Christ, we become like trees planted by streams of living water—strong, vibrant, and fruitful. Our lives begin to reflect his love and grace, and others will be drawn to the light of Christ within us. Through us, God's encouragement can flow to others, offering them hope and pointing them to his truth.

Dear God, help me to be firmly planted in you.
Let my roots grow deep in your truth,
and keep my heart focused on your Word.
May my life reflect your love,
bearing fruit that honors you.
In Jesus's name, I pray.

February 29

LET THE HOLY SPIRIT BE YOUR DAILY PLANNER

So don't worry about tomorrow,
for tomorrow will bring its own worries.
Today's trouble is enough for today.
~ Matthew 6:34

For years, every night, I have created a to-do list for the next morning. I'd joke with my family and tell them I do all this because I'm a reincarnated Martha of the Bible, always busy and moving.

The truth is, I make these lists because I believe if I can see what's ahead, I'll stay on task and accomplish everything. Yet, no matter how well I plan, life always goes awry, and my perfect schedule often crumbles by midday.

This used to frustrate me until I realized something: my plans aren't always God's plans. I had been so focused on staying in control of my day that I forgot who truly holds the reins. The Holy Spirit gently reminded me that God has already planned each day before I even open my eyes in the morning. His plans are better than anything I could map out for myself, even if I can't see the bigger picture.

God's only requirement for us is simple: stay in touch with him. When we focus on him, rather than obsessing over our agendas, he leads us through each moment with grace. There's incredible peace in entrusting our day to the Holy Spirit. By letting him guide our steps, we free ourselves from the burden of worrying about tomorrow and can embrace the blessings of today.

Lord, thank you for already guiding my days
and watching over me.
Help me to surrender my plans to you
and let the Holy Spirit guide my steps.
Teach me to focus on today
and trust you with
tomorrow.

Endnotes

DECEMBER 7

1. Kim M. Clark, *Deep Waters: Lift Your Gaze* (Deep Waters Books, 2018), 86.

DECEMBER 18

1. C. S. Lewis, *The Last Battle* (HarperTrophy, 2001), 128.

DECEMBER 25

1. "Nicene Creed," Christian Classics Ethereal Library, accessed April 21, 2025, https://www.ccel.org/creeds/nicene.creed.html.

JANUARY 1

1. Billy Graham, *Hope for Each Day: Words of Wisdom and Faith* (Thomas Nelson, 2017), 382.

JANUARY 7

1. William D. Barrick and Roger Sigler, "Hebrew and Geologic Analysis of the Chronology and Parallelism Hebrew and Geologic Analysis of the Chronology and Parallelism of the Flood: Implications for Interpretation of the Geologic Record," accessed May 6, 2024, https://digitalcommons.cedarville.edu/icc_proceedings/vol5/iss1/29/.

JANUARY 10

1. "A Model Church," Open the Bible, accessed May 14, 2024, https://openthebible.org/open-the-bible-daily/a-model-church/.

JANUARY 24

1. 1. Edward Mote, "My Hope is Built on Nothing Less," Hymnary, accessed July 3, 2024, https://hymnary.org/text/my_hope_is_built_on_nothing_less.

FEBRUARY 5

1. "Billy Graham Once Detested Church," CBN, accessed September 12, 2024, https://www2.cbn.com/news/us/billy-graham-once-detested-church-main-prayer-his-mother-prayed-him.
2. "Billy Graham > Quotes > Quotable Quote," Goodreads, accessed September 12, 2024, https://www.goodreads.com/quotes/7484385-i-have-never-known-a-man-who-received-christ-and.

FEBRUARY 7

1. "Sarah Young > Quotes > Quotable Quote," Goodreads, accessed March 27, 2025, https://www.goodreads.com/quotes/1216800-i-the-creator-of-the-universe-am-with-you and Nicholas Patrick Wiseman, *The Dublin Review, Volume 2* (London: William Spooner, 1837), https://books.google.com/books?id=z9EsAQAAIAAJ&%20q=%22leads+men%22#v=snippet&q=%22leads%20men%22.

About the Author

You'll find Debb Joy either reading her Bible or playing the piano in her spare time after she completes her exercise and house chores. That is, after she's loved on her pets.

Debb loves cooking for family and everyone else who graces her doorstep. When stressed, you'll find her furiously digging in her garden, cleaning, or on the treadmill. She continually goes into her prayer closet, the war room at church, and her Wednesday morning Bible Studies to petition her Savior for the needs of the Kingdom. She loves texting out her devotionals to a long list of 500+ truckers and friends across the nation.

Debb loves surrounding herself with her favorite people: her husband Kerry, daughter Madolyn, son-in-love Chris, and her two handsome grandsons. Find her at www.debbjoy.com.

About the Illustrator

Madolyn Phillips was practically born with a crayon in her hand. From her earliest days, creativity has been second nature, and though she isn't a professional graphic designer, she delights in anything that allows her to make art. Her illustrations shine throughout her mother's devotional series, *Coffee with God and Joy in the Mornings*, where her vibrant touch brings the words to life.

Madolyn proudly boasts that her family is the true love of her life— her devoted husband and two grown sons. She's also the heartbeat of our extended family fun, leading the charge on river rafting trips, Fourth of July picnics, Oktoberfest celebrations, and countless other adventures that keep everyone close.

Want to Keep Going?

Enjoyed your *Coffee with God and
Joy in the Winter Mornings:
90 Sips of Strong Grace, Bold Faith,
and Endless Mercy?*

Grab a copy of all of Debb Joy's seasonal devotionals.
Go to www.debbjoy.com for more information.

More Publications by
Deep Waters Books

For more fine books published by Deep Waters Books
go to www.deepwatersbooks.com or
scan the QR code below:

DEEP WATERS BOOKS